MOUNTAIN CLIMBERS ARE PRIVILEGED!

"The techniques of mountain climbing are interesting, for they allow a person to enter into wide and dramatic areas. A man or woman can stand on a high peak far above the flights of eagles and high above the cry of the marmot. You can look below and see clouds piling up against cliffs. You can watch peaks appear and disappear in storms. Or you can see above them the bluest skies on earth. At night, thousands of stars are revealed that are never seen any place else on earth. . . .

"The essence of this book is really about the joys and wonders of mountain climbing. . . . However, mountain climbing is mainly a technical sport. You must know about ropes, pitons, ice axes, tents, crampons, and so forth before attempting any climb. But remember, as you read what is written about equipment and techniques, that the end result is the emotional reward.

"All is written so that you may safely find in the mountains that which you seek."

—Howard E. Smith, Jr.

THE COMPLETE BEGINNER'S GUIDE TO MOUNTAIN CLIMBING

Howard E. Smith, Jr.

Illustrated with photographs and with drawings by Griffith Jones

POCKET BOOKS, a Simon & Schuster division of
GULF & WESTERN CORPORATION
1230 Avenue of the Americas, New York, N.Y. 10020

Published by arrangement with Doubleday & Company, Inc.
Library of Congress Catalog Card Number: 76-18366

ISBN: 0-671-82071-0

First Pocket Books printing May, 1978

1 2 9 8

Printed in the U.S.A.

Acknowledgment

The author wishes to express his gratitude to Dr. Andrew Spielman for his generosity of time and spirit in making comments on the manuscript of this book.

Dedication

This book is dedicated
to all of my friends of the
Colorado College Mountain Club.

Contents

Preface

The techniques of mountain climbing are interesting, for they allow a person to enter into wide and dramatic areas. A man or woman can stand on a high peak far above the flights of eagles and high above the cry of the marmot. You can look below and see clouds piling up against cliffs. You can watch peaks appear and disappear in storms. Or you can see above them the bluest skies on earth. At night, thousands of stars are revealed that are never seen any place else on earth. Brilliant wildflowers grow, thriving from the waters of melted snows. Ptarmigans, those fat grouse which are white in the winter and stone-gray in the summer, may walk right up to climbers and stare up at them. Thus, mountain climbers are privileged.

At other times, thanks again to technical skills, climbers can climb high cliffs and look thousands of feet down over snow and slanting rocks to a glacier far below. They can stand where no one has ever stood before. They can listen to the high ringing notes of a piton being pounded into cracks above them. They can experience the thrill and excitement of difficult mountain climbing.

As a sport, mountain climbing has many things to offer. Like any interesting sport it calls for many skills. Only a person who understands the skills and who has practiced them can ever be a good or reliable mountain climber. Thus it is always a challenge to learn more and be more proficient. In terms of teamwork, mountain climbing is the ultimate sport, for in no other sport does one rely so much on another person. No mountain is climbed alone, but by a team. Like most sports, mountain climbing is a physical sport requiring not only strength and stamina but balance and grace as well. Few sports rival it for developing judgment. Climbers are forced, at all times, to judge rocks, routes, and weather, to say nothing of assessing the strengths and weaknesses of their own climbing party. They must also figure out a strategy for climbing difficult pitches and high peaks.

Unfortunately, mountain climbing is also a relatively dangerous sport. But so are many others. Some, such as skiing, swimming, and motorcycle racing may be more dangerous. You can certainly say, however, that climbing always presents risks, and especially for beginners.

It is this feature of danger which made me, personally, wonder whether or not to write a book on mountain climbing, for it is not my purpose to encourage people to participate in any risky sport. On the other hand, the risk is there whether anyone writes about it or not. It is best not to sweep things under the rug. People will climb mountains anyway, and it is better to help them do it safely.

This book, I hope, will help in its own way to reduce the risk for anyone who reads it and enable him to climb cliffs and mountains as safely as possible. After all, more and more people are going into the hills every day. It is amazing to see the increase in the number of climbers in the last few years. If this book can help them, then it will have done its duty.

Of course, no one can ever learn mountain climbing from a book, and that certainly should be clear from the beginning. No one in his right mind would read a book on ocean sailing and set off on a solo voyage around the world. This book, therefore, should be used only as an aid. The real lessons should come from an experienced mountain climber. A beginner should contact one through mountain clubs. Or most stores supplying mountain climbing equipment to the public can tell a person about climbers he can contact.

Though there are practical (and not-so-practical) reasons for mountain climbing which have to do with developing the body and mind, there are also reasons which have to do with the emotions, the psyche, even the spirit. Mountains frequently give us a sense of freedom and power. The experience of being in the high mountains often increases our feeling of awareness. Many people are awed by the solitude of the mountains. For others the risks themselves seem to make them suddenly and intensely conscious of their lives in such a way that they see themselves as total persons. Some people seem suddenly to open up to new experiences, new sights, new sensations. It is a rare person who is not deeply affected by the mountain regions of the world.

The essence of this book is really about the joys and wonders of mountain climbing. Every sentence I wrote called to mind the deeper values. However, mountain climbing is mainly a technical sport. You must know about ropes, pitons, ice axes, tents, crampons, and so forth before attempting any climb. But remember, as you read what is written about equipment and techniques, that the end result is the emotional reward. All is written so that you may safely find in the mountains that which you seek.

THE COMPLETE BEGINNER'S GUIDE TO MOUNTAIN CLIMBING

1

How to Walk

Mountain climbing is a walking sport. To do it, you must know how to walk correctly. The type of hiking needed is very different from that normally encountered on a city street or even along trails. You are often carrying a heavy pack through rugged country, off trails, in areas of broken ground, over boulder fields, and in other areas of difficult terrain. Such walking calls for new skills.

In mountainous areas it is important to walk in such a way that you are always balanced. Most people put one foot in front of the other as they walk and more or less fall toward it, slamming it down on the ground. In climbing, you should walk the way the American Indians did. At any given time an Indian was balanced. Thus, if you can imagine freezing him into a statue, he would be perfectly balanced. No matter at what point in his step the statue was made, you could balance it with one foot off the ground.

You may wonder why it is necessary to walk that way. There are reasons. First, it is much less tiring, because it is more natural and graceful. You do not "pound" your foot as you walk and jolt your bones and muscles. Another reason has to do with the terrain. Quite often a climber is walking on or near loose boulders. On them you must keep your balance. Many boulders roll or tilt. You cannot go "slamming" into them. If you are always balanced while walking on boulders, you can back away from an unsteady place before you have put your full weight on it. This holds true of logs and other unsteady objects as well. Most of all, balanced walking gives you a true sense of control over all of your motions.

In walking in a graceful, balanced way, you roll your hips a bit. In other words, you do not walk in a mechanical manner like a metal robot. As you roll slightly from side to side, you get more spring out of your effort. Not only does this give you a stronger stride but it conserves energy. Walking is a matter of feel. A good hiker feels free. He feels the spring, looseness, and delicacy of each step. A ballet dancer gets a sense of enjoyment from dancing, and so should a hiker from hiking correctly.

When you are walking up a steep incline, you can save energy by using the lock-knee method of hiking. Most people walking up stairs will walk up them with knees bent. Thus, the weight of the body is carried on tense muscles.

Here is how to climb by the lock-knee method. Let us assume you are standing upright at the base of some stairs. Both feet are together. You push back with your knees until they go no further backward. From that position you take a step. As you do so, you keep the knee of the supporting leg straight and the knee "locked." You place the other foot up on the next stair. You raise yourself. Once both feet are at the same height, you quickly lock the other knee, and continue. Thus, most of the time your weight is carried straight down through the bones of your legs. This method helps a great deal, especially if you have a pack. On each step the muscles have a chance to relax for a moment.

Most people who first try the lock-knee method find it boring and artificial, if not awkward. It is best to practice it before going on a hike. You can learn it on stairs. As awkward as it may seem at first, you will begin to learn to do it automatically.

Downhill walking on steep slopes, especially when you are weighted down with a pack, can be a problem. All the weight pushes you in an uncomfortable and awkward way. Before going down a steep hill, see that the laces on your boots are a bit tighter than usual. The pressure from the weight can hurt your toes by pushing them against the front of the boots. Tighter laces will help hold the foot back. Downhill walking will test the knee muscles. Be extra careful. You are prone to slips, a tumble, or a twisted knee. Never leave a good trail and take short cuts straight down a steep slope. On a long downhill trail, rest periodically. This will prevent your muscles from "giving out." Never rush down a long, sloping trail.

Most mountain climbers are forced, at one time or another, to cross scree slopes. These are slopes that are deeply covered with small pebbles varying in size and shape. Some are rocks the size of rice grains and some are the size of walnuts. The slopes are made up from weathered rocks. The characteristic of scree slopes is that they all "give." As you walk on a scree slope, the rock particles give way under you. It is the old three steps forward and two backwards.

In crossing a scree slope, move rather rapidly in easy strides. Keep the body perpendicular. Do not lean in toward the slope. What you want to do is to keep the weight of your body straight down toward the feet so they get as much traction as possible. The more you lean in toward the slope, the less weight there is holding your feet on the ground.

If you are going down a scree slope, the weight of the body will push the scree downward. Once the scree starts moving, move off of it. The longer you are on it, the faster it can start to roll. The trick is to use the inertia of the gravel. Land on it before it gets into motion and get off it before it moves too far and too fast.

To climb some mountains, a climber must cross large boulder fields. If the boulders are really large, you can leap gracefully from one to the next. This is frequently called "boulder hopping." The trick, once again, is to land on a boulder and move off of it before it has a chance to tilt. The heavier the boulder the more inertia it will have. This, of course, is dangerous. The safer way is to move painstakingly from one boulder to the next, testing each as you go. Actually, most large boulder fields are crossed using both methods. Much of it depends on how tired you are and how much experience you have. A beginner should not boulder hop. Furthermore, he should take frequent rests if needed. Crossing a boulder field is tiring work.

Some mountains have rather steep slopes covered with boulders that move together when a climber walks across them. Stay away from such places, as they are extremely dangerous.

When you are walking in the mountains, you will frequently be walking on slopes of hard rock. Obviously, the steeper the slope the more difficult it is to stand on. Always stand straight up; do not lean in toward it. As with a scree slope, the feet will have less and less traction the more you lean toward the slope. When walking up steep mountain slopes, be careful to be aware of the steepness of the slope. Most slopes are not even in steepness.

On any slope or ledge watch out for loose gravel over hard rock. Gravel can act like ball bearings under your feet and make it easy to slip. Grass can be extremely slippery. In fact, in California some children make cardboard sleds and slide down grassy slopes. Of course, in hiking never depend on trees or bushes for support. A tree can be rotten inside and look perfectly all right outside. Do not, if you can help it, walk above high cliffs and drop-offs. This is especially true if there is a high wind. If you are near a cliff, do not throw rocks off it. Such an action can throw you off balance.

On any long hike you must walk at a steady pace. The process is somewhat difficult to describe, for pace is something one "feels." However, you can say that the mountain climber's pace is slower than others. A backpacker walking on a relatively level trail should walk slowly enough so that his breathing will not interfere with a conversation. If he is panting so much that he cannot talk to his companions, he is walking too fast. While that is a fairly good rule for such hiking, the conditions will vary a great deal.

A steady slow pace that calls for few rest stops is far better than one that is faster but requires more resting. You should be able to walk about an hour without needing a rest. This includes steep climbing where you are panting for breath.

Some good climbers say you should be able to hike without a rest for even longer periods of time, maybe two or three hours. There is a lot to be said for that. If you can hike through the mountains for two or three hours without stopping and without tiring too much, it proves that you are in good shape and know what you are doing. You have strength and stamina, and can also keep track of your heartbeat and breathing. However, all that takes practice and calls for experience. The beginner needs some sort of guidelines.

First, try to hike about an hour on level ground and not get out of breath. If you do begin to pant, slow down.

On a steep grade try to keep your breathing in control. If it is a bit uncomfortable but is not getting worse, you are probably okay. In each case, walk about an hour, then rest for about ten minutes. Sit down and take it easy. Have a drink. Nibble on something. If you find that you need to rest more often than once an hour, you are walking too fast. If you must rest every half hour or more frequently it is a sign that you are either too tired and weak or that you are pushing too hard.

On the other hand there is no cut-and-dried rule. If you are within a mile of the summit of a high peak and you are resting every twenty minutes, you may still be able to reach your goal.

Thus, in a sense it depends on where you are. As a rule of thumb, one can say that early in the day, at low altitudes, you should not rest more than once an hour and your pace should be steady and easy. At the end of the day, near a high summit, you may be forced to rest much more often.

Pick resting spots with some care. Psychologically it is better to rest at the top of a steep grade than at the bottom of it. Try to pick a scenic place to rest, so you can enjoy it more. Also, rest spots are good places to take photographs. Such activities take your mind off of your weary bones. If you are aching or feel cramped, you might take some salt tablets, for those symptoms may indicate a loss of salt. The more you perspire, the more salt you lose. Try not to rest in a cold, windy spot, as the cold air may tighten up your muscles.

Try to stay comfortable at all times. Do not wear tight fitting clothes. Do not get cold, but, on the other hand, do not be dressed too warmly. Try to be just a slight bit on the cool side.

It is very difficult for hikers in mountainous regions to know how long it will take to go from one place to another. On level land near sea level on a good summer day, it is usually easy to tell how long it will take to hike ten miles. In the mountains it is often next to impossible to say how long it will take to hike ten miles. A great deal of it has to do with the terrain. Cold weather and snow can slow climbers down. Indeed, deep snow and high winds in sub-zero weather can make some mountains virtually impossible, even mountains which in the summer would be considered easy to climb.

The solitude of the mountains and their wild, untamed aspects appeal to climbers. (*Courtesy Swiss National Tourist Office*)

As a rule of thumb, a beginner should probably not consider hiking more than twelve miles in one day on a trail which gains over 3,000 feet in altitude. The temperature should not be below freezing, nor should there be any problems such as deep snow on the ground, boulder fields, and so on. Even for such a one-day trip, you should build up to it, especially if the beginning of the trail is already at a high altitude. It would be best to take a short two-mile hike a day before. Get in shape slowly.

Mountain climbing is different from any other sport, for it takes place at high altitudes where there is less air to breathe. Most people feel a little difficulty in breathing at 9,000 feet. Airplane pilots need extra oxygen at over

10,000 feet above sea level. No one lives permanently at altitudes of 18,000 feet above sea level. Mountain climbers often carry oxygen tanks and wear oxygen masks at extreme altitudes, though Mount Everest, 29,002 feet above sea level, was climbed without oxygen masks.

The trick to breathing at high altitudes is to get as much air into the lungs as possible. Our lungs are in the cavity of our chest. To bring air into them, we lower the diaphragm at the base of the chest. Muscles control it. Oddly enough, most people have a mistaken idea of what a deep breath really is. When someone is asked to take a deep breath he will expand the upper part of his chest. But that is *not* a deep breath. In a deep breath the air goes deep down into the chest. The chest expands somewhat, but more to the point, the "stomach" area looks as though it were expanding. You can tell if you take a deep breath. Put your hand slightly above your navel. Now take a deep breath. Your hand should move noticeably outward. When a mountain climber is panting, his abdomen looks as though it were heaving in and out.

A person who is planning to go mountain climbing should practice the correct way to breathe. He should take in deep breaths and have them go way down. Even the "stomach" should move. Do not overdo it by breathing rapidly and deeply for too long, as that can be dangerous. However, get the idea of it and be able to take really deep breaths.

Because you breathe deeply in the mountains, you have to be sure not to constrict the waist. Wear a belt low and do not hang things from it.

Many people suffer from mountain sickness at higher elevations. It has definite symptoms. Often you will feel completely lazy. A few people feel nauseated and get headaches. But for elevations up to about 20,000 feet you can get used to the altitude, and the symptoms will go away. Most people can adjust in three or four days. Thus, if you are going to a region of high altitudes, do not plan to do much for the first five days.

But the human body never completely adjusts. At higher altitudes you often need more sleep. Even at an elevation of 7,000 feet most people sleep about forty minutes longer a night. At elevations over about 22,000 feet the body cannot adjust at all. From that elevation on up the body continues to be starved for oxygen. In truth, one is slowly dying at such elevations. That is why mountain climbers often wear oxygen masks on very high peaks.

Many athletic people who can do so much at lower altitudes are surprised at the shortness of breath experienced during a difficult climb over 10,000 feet. Each thousand feet is progressively more difficult. A person struggling up a mountain may feel very distressed by the lack of air. Several things may happen. Some people think that they can rush the peak. They want to hurry up and get it all over with before they become too exhausted. Though it is obvious such an idea will not work, many beginners fall prey to such a notion. Others may call for more and more frequent rests. Some people will flop down into the snow, utterly exhausted. It is better for them to slow down.

Experienced mountain climbers expect to have difficulties and painful breathing and put up with it. The beginner should realize that on a high mountain he will be in pain. The higher the mountain, the more he will hurt. By realizing it will occur and by breathing correctly and pacing himself, he can cut it down a great deal.

2

Boots

One of the most important items a mountain climber will buy is his pair of boots. When you select them be very careful. Start thinking about them in the most basic way. Why is there a need for boots? Obviously you are buying boots to protect your feet from cold weather. In addition, boots cover the feet and ankles so that sharp rocks will not cut them and the toes won't be twisted by roots.

Furthermore, boots are needed to give extra support to the whole foot. This is especially important when a climber is carrying a heavy pack. Though you can walk around barefoot comfortably, you cannot carry a heavy load barefoot, especially if you do it for only two weeks out of the year. The ankles and feet cannot develop strong enough muscles in such a short time to carry the extra weight. So a climber will look for support, leather heavy enough to protect the feet from bruises and cuts, and room enough for warm socks.

A mountain climber has several types of shoes to consider. There are, roughly speaking, three types. One is a lightweight shoe designed for rock climbing. It can also be used for hiking short distances without a heavy pack. One type lightweight is called a kletterschuh. The others are medium-weight hiking boots for general hiking on trails, and a heavyweight boot for more rugged conditions. You should first decide what sort of mountain climbing you will be doing, then get the right sort of boot for the activity.

Rock climbing boots and kletterschuhs are light in weight. All have rubber soles for gripping the rock. One type has a smooth sole, somewhat like a tennis shoe. These

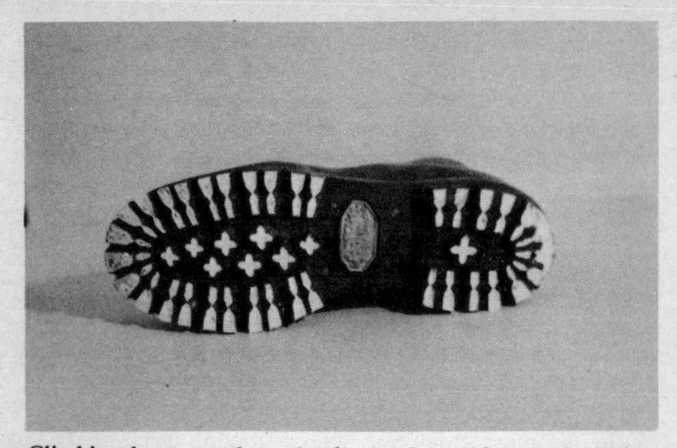

Climbing boots need good soles, such as this one, for gripping rock. (*Photograph by Alexander Smith*)

soles are good only on rock, and no good at all on grass, wet slopes, and other areas. In fact, they are dangerous. The other type of boot has a lug sole. These are soles with deep cuts and high ridges. They grip on most things far better than smooth soles. Rock climbing boots are ankle high so that the ankle and calves can have freedom of motion. The soles of lightweight boots are cut very close to the boot itself so that there is a lack of leverage when one is standing on a very narrow ledge.

There are also heavyweight rock climbing boots. They have all the above features, except, of course, that they are heavier and more rugged. The soles differ though. They are very stiff. The reason for this is that, once the foot is placed in a foothold, the boot will not move out of place so easily. Also one can jam a stiff-soled boot into a crack more easily.

Some boots combine various features. There are some relatively lightweight boots with stiff soles.

The medium-weight hiking boot is made for general trail use. The heavier a boot is on your feet, the more tiring it will be to "carry" it around. Some people say a pound of boot equals five on the back, but that would depend on the individual. At any rate, the medium-weight boot is a compromise between a heavy, powerful almost nondestructible boot and a lightweight boot which will not offer enough strength and support. The sole of the medium-

Medium-weight hiking and climbing boot. (*Photograph by Alexander Smith*)

weight boot is heavy enough so that the hiker, loaded down with a pack, will not feel small stones on the trail. If he does, his feet can be bruised.

The heavyweight boot is made for off-the-trail hiking. It is also constructed for ice and snow work. Most are insulated against cold weather. It is strictly a boot for a person expecting the worst in terms of rocks, glaciers, and ice.

From the above descriptions you can pretty well decide what you want. Obviously, beginners can generally forget about heavyweight boots. Those who will be doing mostly trail hiking and some not-too-difficult rock climbing will probably end up getting a medium-weight boot, which is probably the most practical for the beginning mountain climber. If, however, you are not going on any long hikes and are only going to do rock climbing, then you should choose a rock climbing boot. The best is probably a rather lightweight one with a stiff sole. Beginners should choose in any boot one which is ankle high and which has lug soles.

Many boots offer arch support. Some people like it, some do not. I, personally, like it. I have high arches and like to feel that they are supported high and won't go down.

Select boots which do not constrict the ankles. Most mountain boots today are about six inches high. The

Achilles' tendon should not be tightly bound. If it is, it will ache. Moreover, the wearer will get blisters. Many boots have padding at the top to protect the tendon. However, a boot does not have to be padded to fit well there.

Another reason for not having high boots is so that air can circulate down into the boot. You will wear woolen socks. Air can move downward through them. When you take a step, air is pushed up out of the socks. When you lift your foot once more, air seeps back in. If the boot is much higher, this process will not take place and your feet will be damper.

Be sure that the boots are made of good material. Nothing beats real leather. Most good boots are made of either steer or horsehide leather. The boots may be lined, though this is not absolutely necessary. Investigate the workmanship as carefully as you can. Good boots look well made. Good boots for mountain climbing have as few seams as possible. This is because a seam is a natural weak point, and the more there are, the more weak points there are. Yet my personal experience has been that boots wear out in other ways first.

Hiking boots should not have pointed toes. The boot tops should never sag in such a way that they rub against the top of the foot or on the toes.

The fit of the boot is of great importance. When you are buying boots, take your time and see to it that the boot fits well. Before trying on a pair of boots, put on two pairs of socks—a light pair of cotton or silk socks and then a pair of woolen socks. Wear new socks, as they are a bit more bulky than an old pair. These are what you will be wearing on the trail and you want to know how the boot will feel with them on.

Boot sizes are to some degree less than accurate. Thus, one marked 10-D may really be a 10-C. The last, or shape of the shoe, may have more to do with how the boot feels than the actual size of the boot. It is best not to be influenced by marked sizes.

When you first try on a boot, before you lace it up stick your finger down the heel and see if there is room back there for your finger. The reason is that when you lace up the boot, the laces will pull your heel back in place, almost up against the back of the boot. When that happens it is obvious that there is a finger's width of room up in front between the toes and front of the boot. On shoes you can sometimes push down through the soft leather and feel where your toes are, but with some mountain climbing boots that is impossible. Even then, you still want to make sure the toes will not be cramped. Kick the boot forward hard against something like a wall or post and find out if your toes slide forward and touch the front of the boot. If they do, get another pair.

Next, see how the boot feels across the widest part of your foot, over the ball of the foot. When you walk, especially with a heavy pack, your feet should spread outward. That place should not be too tight. Be careful of the location of your little toe and big toe against the side of the boot. They should not be cramped. What a person should seek is support across the front of the boot, but the support must also allow room for the toes and for the foot to spread in normal walking. In other words, it is support without any tightness. Of all things to test, that is one of the most difficult. Yet it must be done. If the boot is too tight, the foot will tire quickly and feel cramped. If there is too much room, the foot can slip around and get blisters. One way of checking is to curl your toes back under. If you can do so, it is a sign that perhaps it is not too tight. However, it is not a final test.

When your foot is in the boot, try to determine if the foot points straight forward normally as it would if you were barefoot. The boot should not "turn" the foot into an unnatural position. The wrong last can do that.

Check the heel. The boot should grip it gently, holding it in place. This is usually the easiest part of fitting. See that the boot above the heel does not rub into the Achilles' tendon.

When the boot is laced up, look at the laces. There should be some tongue showing under them. If the uppers touch with the boots laced you will not have any extra space to use. Later, you may never be able to get them laced tightly enough.

When choosing the boots, try on several different pairs. Since all new boots and shoes feel odd at first, you want to know if the boot feels odd because it is new or because it really does not fit quite right. Compare. Take your time. If needed, spend a few afternoons trying boots on.

Most salesmen who sell regularly to hikers and mountain climbers try to be helpful. If you have any questions, ask. Most salesmen know what they are doing, and it is usually best to listen to what they have to say.

Do not think that you can "break in" a pair of boots. If they do not fit properly at first, they will never fit properly. No faults, except for some stiffness, can ever be worked out. When you find a pair that seem okay, put both boots on and walk around in the store. Check any slight pinch any place where the boot rubs against the foot. If there is any problem, choose another pair. If the boots feel good, rub your hand across them, pushing the leather and see how much give there is. In a lightweight and even a medium-weight boot there should be some give on the top of the foot. Some heavier boots will not give at all, so the test cannot be made. Walk around once more. Go up on your toes. Twist your foot. Curl your toes. Make every foot motion you can. If all tests have been passed, buy the boots.

Never go on a hike with boots less than three weeks old. Once you get your boots, ask the salesman how to take care of them and how to waterproof them. After that, wear the boots as much as you can. But, start slow. On the first day wear them about an hour and a half with two pairs of socks. Take off the boots and socks. Check your feet very carefully for any starting blisters. Look for red marks or chafed areas. If there are some starting and they do not look serious, then wear other boots or shoes for most of the day. Many hours later put the boots on once more. Wear them around for another hour. Even if no redness or any other sign appears, it would be best to leave them off after that. On the next day wear them for maybe three hours. Again make a careful check. If all is all right, then wear them almost all day the third day. If everything is fine then, wear them all day from then on. Wear them to the movies and out for the evening.

Good boots need minimum care. Oil or wax the boots every now and then during the summer and more during the winter. Do not stuff your socks down into them at night. Boots should dry out. In a cabin or tent they can be placed on the floor. Outdoors at night the best way to store them is upside down over sticks. If it rains, the water will not fill up the boots. Watch out for animals, especially porcupines. They may decide the boots will make a nice salty meal. If porcupines are around, hang the boots upside down from a line on a branch out of the animals' reach.

Many people make the mistake of drying boots near fires or heaters. Since boot leather is a type of skin, a flame too warm for your hand or foot will be too warm for the boots. You would never leave the bare skin of your foot near a heater all night long. The boot cannot take it either. Many a pair of boots has been ruined that way.

A cold, soggy, wet pair of boots which will function are much better than cracked, ruined, dry boots that have been near the campfire all night.

When you go hiking, you should wear two pairs of socks. Next to the skin wear a pair of real silk socks—a real luxury indeed. Over them place a pair of medium-heavy wool socks. The silk socks next to the skin keep the feet protected from the wool socks. Moreover, the wool socks slide over them. If the wool socks can slide back and forth and not build up heat or friction against the skin, they will not cause blisters. Silk is best, because wool slides most on it. Also, silk in itself is warm and it conducts water away from the skin. The next best substitute for silk is cotton. Never use socks of nylon or other man-made fibers. They do not lead sweat away from the skin. In fact, sweat builds up under them, softening the skin and causing the feet to blister even more easily.

There are several grades of woolen socks from soft, thin ones to extra heavy, bulky ones. If you are hiking in above-zero weather, the best are medium-heavy, with as few ribs as possible. Very heavy socks tend to ball up. For cold weather, wear two pairs of wool socks, unless they are so thick in the boot that they constrict the foot and circulation to it. Wool is a great material—the only one which will stay warm even when wet. By itself it is somewhat weak though, so choose socks with 10 to 15 per cent nylon. Some socks have nylon reinforced heels. Sometimes the reinforcing goes as high as 40 per cent nylon. A compromise is a sock with 70 per cent wool and 30 per cent nylon. However, with each thread of nylon you lose some wool. So it is all a balance between strength and durability on the one hand and the comfort, protection against cold, and dampness-proofing of wool on the other.

For very cold weather with temperatures below zero and colder, climbers wear a different sort of boot, which fits over their regular boots. These are somewhat like overshoes, but lighter in weight and easier to walk in. They are insulated with polyurethane foam and have aluminum surfaces which reflect some 90 per cent of the heat lost from the foot. These overboots are designed so that one can wear crampons with them. There are other types of boots as well for cold weather. One, used for easy-to-climb mountains, is the shoepac. This is a boot with a rubber bottom and leather top. One can wear socks, plus felt liners in it.

When you are going to be climbing in snow or in places where there are many scree slopes, you may want to wear gaiters. These are cloth leggings which you place over the boot and up over the pants leg so that snow and pebbles do not fall down into the boot. They also help protect that gap between the boot top and pants bottom from cold winds.

The most common foot complaints on the trail are blisters and sprains. You get blisters when your boots or socks do not fit properly. In fact, there is really no other way of getting them. Thus, prevention is the key.

If you do get a blister and it is not about to break and looks as though it will not unless irritated further, cover it with moleskin. This is a soft bandage made just for that purpose. If the blister has opened, or you know it soon will, then open it carefully. The way you do that is to use a sterile needle and prick the base of the bubble and let the liquid in it drain. After all that, put on disinfectant. If there are loose pieces of skin which will further rub more skin, cut them off.

To prevent infection and other problems, always keep your feet clean. First, wear clean socks. White socks are best. If they get dirty, you can see the dirt. After a day's hike, wash your feet. Some climbers carry rubbing alcohol to rub off the grime and to refresh their feet.

3

Mountain Clothing

When considering clothing or sleeping bags, you need to know what the term "loft" means. Loft refers to the thickness of an article of clothing and/or sleeping bag, usually one stuffed with down or Dacron. The thicker a sleeping bag is, the more loft it has. Normally, a down-filled jacket with about 3 inches of loft will be warmer than one only two inches thick.

Loft, in my opinion, is an overrated word. The loft of a piece of clothing or sleeping bag is not the ultimate measure of warmth. The quality of the material, the construction of it, and the type of down used may tell a great deal more. Everything has to be equal, though, before you can really compare the loft of one item with that of another. Since clothing and sleeping bags are made in so many ways, you should consider all the factors, not just the loft.

All mountain climbers need a parka or two. Parkas protect you from the bitterly cold winds of the mountainous regions. A parka is a long jacket that reaches at least to the crotch. My own parka actually reaches to my knees. It also has a hood. All are long sleeved, of course, and can be tightened at the wrist. Except for very long parkas, such as my own, they have a waistband so that they can be tightened at the waist. Thus, with the hood closed and all else tightened up, no air can circulate under it. Most parkas have slash pockets in front so that you can put your hands in them. This helps so much to keep the hands warm that a parka without them should not be considered. Some parkas have the hood and wrists fringed with fur. Of course, to help preserve our wildlife, you should get fake fur. The fur keeps ice from forming around the hood and wrists. It adds some protection and warmth.

Parkas are designed to be windproof. For many years this was accomplished by making parkas of double cloth. The cloth was cotton, very tightly woven and often coated. Since there were two layers, the material effectively protected you from the wind. Today most parkas are made of nylon—a stronger material.

Parkas are not designed to be waterproof, but rather are constructed so the material "breathes." A completely waterproof, airtight parka would be extremely uncomfortable, and would only collect sweat and the dampness of the body. Though not designed for rain, most parkas have an extra layer of cloth in the shoulder area. Snow sometimes collects on the shoulders and if it is not too cold, the snow will melt. Also, ropes pass over the shoulders quite often, and the extra material protects the parka.

In general, there are two types of parkas. One is the shell parka. As its name implies, it is simply a shell. It is always bought several sizes larger than might seem to be necessary. The parka is worn outside—over sweaters, jackets, and all other clothing. Also, it is much easier when you are already dressed up and wearing mittens, to put a large parka on in a high wind. Of the shell parkas, some are pullovers and others have zippers all the way down the front, and often buttons as well, in case the zipper breaks. I prefer the kind that can be completely opened up. It is valuable if you feel too warm.

The other type of parka is the insulated parka. It is designed just like a shell parka but has built-in insulation, either Dacron or down. You can obtain one for a wide range of cold-weather conditions. Some are rated for temperatures down to 80 degrees below zero. The greatest warmth for weight is obtained with the down jackets. In making good ones, the manufacturer must see that the down completely surrounds the body and that there are no thin areas lacking enough down. This is done with tubes and baffles. Dacron jackets do not provide as much warmth for a given weight, but they do have an advantage. If a Dacron jacket gets wet, it can be wrung out and dried and it will still insulate. Also it dries remarkably fast.

In choosing between the various parkas, you must consider what you want. To save weight and escape carrying extra sweaters, most mountain climbers today buy a down

A windproof parka. Notice the hood, which is a must. (*Courtesy Recreational Equipment, Inc.*)

jacket, warm enough for the region they will be climbing in, and then a little extra. In other words, if you are going to be climbing in the Sierra Nevada Mountains when the temperatures normally go to 20 degrees, get one which will provide comfort down to zero. The slight added weight and expense will not matter that much, and you will have the security of knowing you'll always be warm enough. Those climbers who are going into damp, wet regions, such as the Pacific Northwest, should probably choose a Dacron-filled jacket. As for the shell parka, it is such a versatile item that everyone should have one. Even if you buy a good down parka, a shell parka worn over it will help protect it and add warmth because of the lessened wind-chill factor. Also, a shell parka can be worn with other combinations of clothing—over sweaters, jackets, and so on.

Before discussing the right pants to wear, let's mention what not to wear. Shorts are not good for mountain climbing, and that includes lederhosen. You can easily cut your legs on rocks. More important, the weather in any mountainous region can suddenly turn cold and windy. Blue jeans should not be worn. In fact, they are dangerous. Some hikers have died of cold in above-freezing weather because they had on blue jeans. They lack any insulating qualities, especially if soaked by a cold rain. Even if that were not a problem, they are too tight.

So what to wear? Since most mountain climbing takes place in cold weather, the obvious choice is a good pair of woolen pants, loose enough so that you can have freedom of action. The best of all for most purposes is a good pair of knickers. They are the only pants which give you really good knee action. Most Europeans use them, but only a few Americans seem to have spotted their value.

A sturdy wool material is whipcord, usually woven with a double thread. My experience has been that trousers of pure wool do not wear as well as those with nylon or Dacron in them.

A few mountain climbers will be in warm-weather regions, such as deserts, where they will be climbing mesas or rock spires. If you are in a region where the temperatures do not sink much below about 50 degrees, you can wear sturdy cotton and Dacron pants. They should be cut full so that you have good knee action.

Many people wear old clothes when they go hiking or climbing. This is not always a good idea, as old clothes can rip and give way more easily than new ones.

For extremely cold weather you can buy down- or Dacron-filled pants. These are large bulky pants which go over regular ones. For ease in getting them on and off, they zipper along the sides. Some are rated to 80 degrees below zero.

Before buying rainwear, you should think of where you are going to be. In many places you simply do not need rainwear, since it is too cold to rain. In other places the likelihood of rain is very slim. For most trips you can take along a regular rain poncho which covers the body and the pack at the same time. For very rainy areas, such as the Pacific Northwest, you should take along a rain jacket with a hood and rain pants.

There are, in general, two types of ponchos. One is made of plastic and the other of rip-stop nylon. The plastic poncho is absolutely waterproof. It is inexpensive, but it does have drawbacks. First, it rips too easily. Second, because it is so waterproof, it holds in your perspiration. You can be terribly uncomfortable using one. The nylon ponchos are not waterproof. They breathe, though, letting moisture out. The only one I ever liked was the U. S. Army type, which is made of a heavy material with a rubberized coating. They are tough and can take it. However, they are heavier than any other type. For really long trips where you might encounter a great deal of rain, the Army surplus type is probably the best bet.

Rain chaps are easy to make from cheap plastic. Cut the plastic to make two cylinders, one for each leg. A hot iron or tape will seal them. You can also buy them.

The best all-round undershirt is made of "fish-net" material. It provides good insulation because each hole holds a pocket of air which is warmed by body heat. Fish-net underpants are also used, and the principle is the same.

You should wear a scarf to hold in heat when you want to do so.

For most cold-weather mountain climbing I would rather put on heavier trousers than wear long underpants, which I always find make my legs uncomfortable. But I often wear flannel pajama bottoms in fairly cold weather. They provide warmth without hugging my legs all day. For me, cotton thermal underwear never works. First, it is never all that warm. Secondly, it is baggy and heavy and clings too much. The only comfortable long underwear I have ever worn was the kind that was wool on the outside and cotton on the inside or fishnet.

Down parkas, jackets, and vests have to some degree supplanted sweaters. There are, of course, a wide variety of sweaters. For mountain climbing, if you choose sweaters, be sure that they are woolen, tough, and durable. For most conditions, it is best to choose two sweaters, a rather lightweight one and a very warm, bulky one. That way, you can be comfortable over a wide range of temperature conditions. Of course, sweaters used alone are almost useless, as wind pours through the open weave. But under a shell parka they can be surprisingly warm, down to temperatures around zero.

There are endless types of shirts, but only a few are really good for mountain climbing. Do not wear shirts made of nylon, rayon, or any other synthetic material. Such materials do not absorb moisture, which means that sweat will just stick to your body, and you'll feel clammy.

The best material is wool. However, some people cannot stand the feel of wool against their bodies. Also, in hot weather, wool is too warm. I have usually worn two shirts. Next to my skin I wear a good sturdy cotton shirt, with a wool shirt over it. I always see to it that a shirt has two pockets—more would be better—and that it buttons all the way down. All my shirts button all the way, so that I can hike with them completely open and stay cool. Many women hike the same way, with a halter on under the shirt.

Many people like down-filled vests. These are lightweight and are not bulky, yet provide warmth.

Many hikers take gloves along for use around a campfire. They are handy for handling wood, hot items, and so on, preventing both splinters and burns. The best for such purposes are rather heavy leather ones. If hot liquid spills on them, most of it quickly drains off.

For rock climbing you often need two sets of gloves. One is a leather glove or at least one with a leather palm to it. This is used for handling ropes so you do not suffer from burns. The other type of glove is a fingerless woolen one. Such a glove keeps the hand warm and functioning but allows you to feel and grip the rocks.

For cold-weather conditions you need a good pair of mittens. Mittens keep your hands and fingers warmer than gloves. The warmest mittens are down-filled. The next warmest are woolen mittens covered with an outer pair of windproof canvas or nylon cloth. Be sure that they are long enough to cover the wrists. There are blood vessels next to the surface of the wrists, and if the wrist is cool they lose a lot of heat. Two pairs of inexpensive woolen mittens inside a canvas ski mitten have worked at temperatures to thirty below with winds gusting over 100 miles an hour.

If you accidentally lose your mittens, you can put wool socks on over your hands. Mittens and gloves are the most frequently lost articles of clothing.

For cold climates a hat is a must. For general activities a watch cap made of wool is quite good. For colder climates, however, it is not good enough. A good hat is the so-called troopers hat. Most are insulated. They have fake fur ear flaps and a fake fur snap-up visor which covers the forehead. The cap part itself is insulated. A chin strap goes down and keeps it on.

For rock climbing you need a hat without a visor, which can be worn under a helmet. Again, the watch cap is good. Some climbers like berets, especially if they are large enough to be pulled down over the ears.

For summer hiking and mountain climbing the best hat, perhaps, is the "crushable" felt one with a brim around it. The brim shades the eyes and can also hold mosquito netting—an important consideration in some areas. The crown of the hat keeps off the hot sun. By the way, the crown or top of the hat should be a couple of inches above the top of the head so that there is an air space there. Only then will the hat protect you from the sun. With any hat, be sure it has a chin strap so that it does not blow away.

A good scarf made of wool is sometimes handy. In cold weather you can wear it either around the neck or around the stomach, held in place with man's greatest invention, the safety pin.

A big handkerchief is also handy. Buy a bright red one—for possible use as an emergency flag. You can use it as a pot holder, an emergency sling, or as a mask against dust—cowboy style. Of course, you do not use it for your nose. A smaller, regular handkerchief is used for that purpose.

You should have a face mask for very cold, windy weather. Some are made of felt or leather and others are down-filled. They cover the whole face, except for eye holes, a nose hole, and a mouth hole. Some cover the mouth as well. You use a face mask with form-fitting goggles. Thus, nothing is exposed except your mouth and nose. A face mask is not merely a protection against cold weather. It allows you to look directly into winds, which you normally would have to turn away from.

A cagole is something like an extra long and roomy parka. It is so large that you can fit your whole body inside of it. You sit in it with your legs up and the cagole pulled tight by a drawstring at the base. Your arms and hands are also pulled inside it and the sleeves closed. The hood is pulled nearly tight and you breathe through a small hole. Some climbers use them on overnight climbs. At night they bivouac and sit in the cagole.

Take along extra nylon shoelaces.

Your belt should be sturdy, but do not wear one with a big buckle.

A lightweight pair of slippers could give your feet a rest while in camp. Down booties are warm and do the same thing, except that you cannot wear them on rough surfaces. Some slippers are really tough. I wore a pair of men's leather slippers much of the time in the desert among the rocks and cactus, and they lasted for years.

Red or "international orange" outer clothing is often worn for two reasons. In an emergency it is easier to find someone dressed in these colors. Also, these are the only colors to wear if you are climbing during hunting season.

Dark colors absorb more heat from sunlight. White reflects heat. Theoretically, at least, you should be warmer in black clothing. Such effects seem to be minimal at cold temperatures, but are more meaningful for people rock climbing in the desert. There, there is a difference between a white hat and a black one.

Nature lovers may sometimes want to be invisible to wild animals. In forests, green, especially camouflaged green, is best. On snowy slopes, where you may see mountain sheep and other wildlife, a pure white parka should help.

Orange, yellow, and red are the most easily seen. In a forest green disappears. White disappears on snow, but so does blue. In a blue shadow a blue tent will be almost invisible. Of course any grays or browns are difficult to see.

When a climber comes home after a trip, he should have all of his clothing immediately cleaned and repaired. Do not wash wool in detergents, even if you have machine-washables, as they take out the vital oils. Carefully read the instructions on how down clothing should be cleaned. Dacron parkas can be washed in a washing machine.

Since it is next to impossible to clean clothes, except possibly socks, on a trip, always carry enough to have clean underwear and socks. Dirty socks can cause blisters, and dirty underwear can chafe or give you a rash.

Take nylon repair tape along on trips for any cuts in nylon clothing. Carry some safety pins, and needles and thread. And take the right sort of waterproofing oil for boots.

The only thing that you should never repair are socks. If they have holes, do not use them. An attempt to fix up the hole will only give you a blister later on.

In the mountains you are frequently faced with changing weather conditions. Occasionally, even in the middle of winter, the bright sun can make a region much warmer than you would expect. I have seen climbers on Pikes Peak in December with their shirts off, enjoying the sun. Later the same day, however, the temperature dropped to twenty below zero and winds over 100 miles an hour buffeted the peak. The same climbers who had their shirts off only hours before were at the summit, dressed in the heaviest clothing they owned. Never trust mountain weather.

No material itself protects you from the cold. What protects you is trapped air. All warm clothing has within it air spaces. Within the weave of wool, for example, there are thousands of air pockets, and the fuzzier the wool, the more trapped air. Down is remarkable in its ability to trap air. Down is fuzzy and its millions of "hairs" hold air.

There is one other way that clothing can keep you warm. Heat can be reflected. This is why small electric heaters have shiny reflectors in back of them. Aluminum fabrics can reflect heat, too. Some overboots have aluminum reflectors in them to reflect back body heat. Space blankets also have aluminum in them.

The body itself fights to stay warm under cold conditions. The biggest problem for the body is to protect vital organs such as the heart and brain. To do so, it gives them as much warm blood as they need to function. Since there is only so much blood in a body, this means extra blood has to come from somewhere else. Blood will be taken from the feet, hands, legs, and arms to protect the vital organs. The body does this by slowing down the flow of blood to the extremities. Thus, on a cold day your feet and hands may actually and literally have less blood in them. When this happens, they become susceptible to cold temperatures. They can freeze much more easily. In fact, to preserve the heart and brain, the body will sacrifice the feet and hands if needed, even as they begin to freeze.

The secret to dressing for cold weather is to keep the head, which holds the brain, and the torso, which holds the other vital organs, warm. Once they are warm, extra blood will start to flow outward to the feet and hands.

People who have worked outdoors know that one of the best ways to keep their feet warm is to put on a hat.

Sweating is a problem for mountain climbers. The physical effort in mountain climbing will often overheat you. The danger in sweating is that if the sweat freezes on you, you can die. Eskimos know all about this and go to great effort not to sweat. In fact, their fur parkas are open at the bottom. The Eskimo is nude under the parka. Cold air does not move upward under the parka, for cold air is heavier than warm air. What happens is that some mixing does take place and constant ventilation keeps the Eskimo from sweating unless he engages in violent exercise.

Even if you do not die from sweating and cooling down, you might slow down and feel sick. Your muscles can cramp. The more you sweat, the more salt is lost. If too much salt is lost, you must replace it by taking salt tablets.

The time when you will most likely sweat is when it is very cold. A person walking out into the cold weather usually overdresses for it. It is best to dress a little bit on the cool side. If you do begin to sweat, you should open up your clothing. For example, if you untuck your shirt, and undo any waistband belt on your parka, you can be like the Eskimo.

4

The Pack

A mountain climber will need a pack—maybe two or three of them. There are, in general, three types to choose from. There is the small "day pack." There is the rucksack or knapsack used for short trips up to about four or five days. The third is a pack with a frame.

The secret to all packs is that the straps should work and be comfortable. There are two shoulder straps on all packs. To fit properly, they should meet in back, even cross each other. Parallel straps are not as good. The straps should be wide enough to spread the load. All straps should be easily adjustable. Be sure they will stay where you want them.

When you go to buy any pack, look at the straps first and check them out. Put the pack on. See how comfortable it is. You will live with the pack hour after hour on the trail. It must not be uncomfortable. Of course, in a store the pack will be free of weight. Have a friend push down on it. Better yet, ask if you can put something in it. Many stores keep weights around for that purpose. Walk around with the pack on. Try on several and compare.

Packs have evolved in the last few years in one major respect. Until recently, all packs were supported by shoulder straps. Now, however, a few built for heavy loads are designed to place a great deal of the load on the hips. Anyone buying a pack that will carry heavy loads—say, more than twenty per cent of his body weight—should consider one of this type. There is nothing particularly complicated about them. They have a large padded belt which is worn over the hips. When trying on a pack, put the padded belt on and see how it supports. Be sure it is comfortable and is tight enough not to slip downhill. Be sure that the pack is long enough so that most of the weight is on your hips. Have the salesman help you. Be satisfied that the hip belt works and does its job before buying the pack.

Rock climbers, in particular, need a good day pack. The pack should, first of all, fit closely to the back. It should not shift from one side to another. You will be using it in places where a shift in weight could throw you. Thus, day packs for such climbing should hug you. The packs are usually quite small, for you will only be carrying lunch, extra sweaters, and a few things like that. Expensive packs have two or more compartments. It is nice to have one for food and the other for sweaters, but you can pay quite a price for such a small luxury. Expensive rock climbers' packs are usually made of nylon coated to make it rain resistant.

For an overnight trip, you usually carry a rucksack. A rucksack often has metal supports that make a frame. The frame keeps the bag away from the back and helps to keep your back from being poked by sharp items in the bag. Also, it helps keep your back cool, and helps carry the weight.

The bag itself should be roomy. If you do not take too much, just tighten the whole thing down. Most rucksacks have pockets on and in them. Each pocket is handmade and you pay for each one. Zippers, fancy leather covers, and so on also cost more. One thing you may want to have on the bag is a patch of leather to attach crampons to the outside of the bag. Some also have attachments for ice axes.

If you get a bag with pockets, consider how they will be used. One can carry the next snack, another the first aid kit; still another can hold maps and notebook, or a poncho. On the other hand, if you pack a pocketless bag carefully, you can place all those items on the top.

You can use a rucksack for trips of up to four or five days, but when you are on a longer trip, or even a shorter one where you are heavily loaded, you will want a pack frame. A pack frame is usually made of metal, though many are made of wood. Over the frame is a webbing or tight canvas. The webbing goes against your back, and spreads the weight. Shoulder straps take up more weight. There is often a hip belt as well. Today most pack frames have packs built into them. On a homemade pack frame

A climber carrying a pack on a slope of Mount St. Elias, 18,008 feet. Note his other equipment: crampons, ice axe, goggles, overboots, parka, and so on. Only by using the correct equipment properly can a climber ever get to the summit of such a mountain. (*Courtesy the American Alpine Club*)

you can roll your things up in a sleeping bag and strap it to the frame, though, of course, you have to be careful how you do it, and see that it is covered.

Always keep the sack neat. Good housekeeping pays off. In packing one, there are two principles to keep in mind. Put light things in the bottom and heavier things on top. It is easier to carry weight high up on the shoulders. Secondly, place those items you may need quickly near the top of the pack. As much as possible, keep all food together, all sleeping gear together, all medical supplies together, and so on.

There are some items a hiker usually keeps in reach—a drinking cup or canteen, some food to nibble on, the day's lunch, a first aid kit, maps, a sweater, and a poncho. Of course, such items can vary. However, in the morning decide what items need to be reachable. It is a waste of time to realize suddenly that what you want is at the bottom of the pack.

Do not carry crampons inside a pack. The points can rip everything up. Many packs have leather patches sewn on the pack and attachments placed for them. When carrying crampons, place rubber point guards over them. Place the crampons on the pack so that the points face into the pack.

An ice axe is also carried on the outside of the pack. It is carried with its head down, and is secured with thongs or cord. It, too, should have guards placed on it. Of course, a hiker may very well want to walk along using the ice axe as a walking stick. When doing so, have the pick end pointing forward.

Ropes are placed in neat coils and attached to the top of the pack, or placed so that the flap of the pack goes over them. See that the ropes are secured and will not rub against anything, especially metal.

Metal hardware, such as pitons, carabiners, and so forth, can be placed inside the pack. Have them high in it, as they are heavy items. Check any and all hardware to see that it has no rough edges which will tear things in the pack or the pack itself.

Most items are better off inside the pack. An exception is the camera. If you have one, carry it around your neck. It is almost useless if you have to hunt for it. What happens if an elk stands on the trail for a couple of seconds?

Or if you come to one point on the trail and there is a great view of a waterfall? Why even bring a camera unless it is immediately available?

Carry a compass and perhaps a small map in your shirt pocket, plus some waterproof matches and a whistle. Do not carry anything on your belt. Wallets, folding knife, and so on go in the pants pockets.

5

Sleeping Bags

A sleeping bag is designed to keep you warm at night. When thinking about sleeping bags, think "warmth."

Mountainous regions are almost always cold. Even in the summer, temperatures in the Colorado Rockies can easily slide to 20° F on an August night. Other regions can be much colder. A mountain climber must be prepared for cold weather. Moreover, temperature readings do not always tell the true story about how cold a place is. If a wind is blowing or the air is damp, you will feel much colder. Several experiments have been done to see how a person feels at certain temperatures when the wind is blowing. This is called the wind-chill factor. The chart shows how you feel at various temperature-wind speed combinations.

The chart does not tell the whole story. Humidity can change it. The temperature of the ground can change it, too.

Most sleeping bag manufacturers rate their sleeping bags. One may say, for instance, that it is comfortable for temperatures from 40° to 0°. When you see such a rating, remember that it is for still air. Thus a bag rated for 40° to 0° may be okay in that range if there is no wind blowing. On the other hand, if you are sleeping in it outside when the temperature is 20° and there is a 25-mile-per-hour wind blowing, the wind-chill factor will be −15° and the sleeping bag will not be warm enough.

Of course, if you sleep in a tent, it will protect you from the wind and you can rely much more on the rating of the sleeping bag. But who always wants to sleep in a tent?

THE WIND CHILL FACTOR

Wind Speed (mph) / Actual Air Temperature	30°F	20°F	10°F	0°F	−10°F	−20°F	−30°F
10	16	2	−9	−22	−34	−45	−58
15	9	−6	−18	−31	−45	−58	−72
20	3	−9	−24	−40	−52	−68	−81
25	0	−15	−29	−45	−58	−75	−89
30	−2	−18	−33	−49	−63	−78	−94
35	−4	−20	−35	−52	−67	−83	−98
40	−4	−21	−36	−54	−69	−84	−101

The wisest course, in my opinion, is to buy a sleeping bag which is rated for much lower temperatures than you expect ever to encounter, including the wind-chill factor. Such sleeping bags are a little more expensive. You cannot afford to be too cold at night. If you are cold at night, it is difficult, if not impossible, to sleep. You lose efficiency. Under extreme conditions that can be dangerous.

Before choosing a sleeping bag, think of the region where you will be mountain climbing, as well as the time of year. Find out how cold it ever gets there at that time of the year. Look at the wind-chill chart and consider the fact that you may sleep outside in 40-mile-an-hour winds, and choose a sleeping bag which will keep you warm at that temperature and a little lower. If you sleep "cold" and the climate you are going into is damp, then choose a sleeping bag which is rated even a bit lower. That way you will have peace of mind, knowing you can take comfortably anything the weather can throw at you.

A mountain climber needs either a down-filled sleeping bag or a Dacron-filled one. No other filler materials are worth considering. Many people think that down consists of feathers. In one respect that is true, but down is quite different from ordinary feathers. It is much fuzzier and lacks the stiff inner spine. Down grows next to some birds' skin. It is in a way like the wool which some dogs grow under the hairs of their coats. The best down in the world comes from eider ducks, but they are near extinction. The next best down comes from geese and is called goose down.

Sleeping bag manufacturers have to make down bags in such a way that the down stays in place in the bag. To keep the down evenly distributed, it is usually placed in tubes and the tubes sewn together. To keep it from shifting around inside the tubes, baffles are sewn into them. In looking at sleeping bags, it is important to see how the tubes are placed and how well the sewing was done.

There are several ways of placing the tubes. Only the very poorest bags are simply sewn together as shown in the first drawing. Such bags obviously leave a place where there is no down. At such a point heat from your body will leak away and you will feel cold. In the other constructions the down is held evenly.

Down is strange in the sense that it can "leak" through most materials. The manufacturer must choose a material which holds the down. The most used material is nylon taffeta. The material holds the down but also allows the sleeping bag to breathe. This is important, for your sweat and your breath cause the inside of the bag to be damp. The dampness must escape or you will wake up wet. Even nylon taffeta is not perfect, for a few sprigs of down will escape now and then.

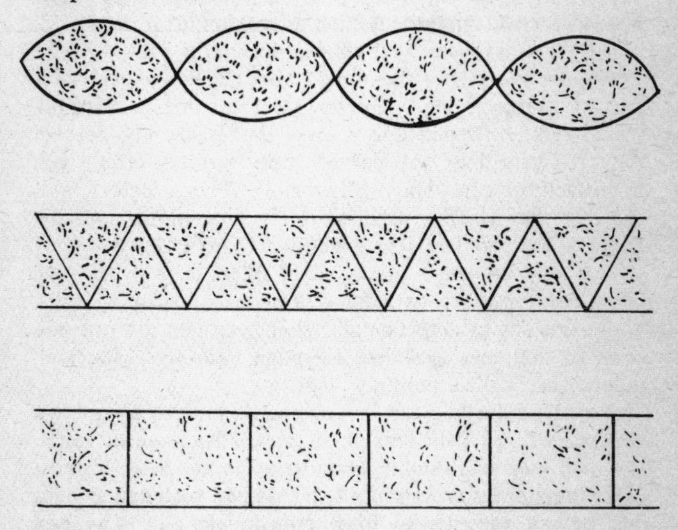

Methods for sewing sleeping bags. In the top illustration, the two pieces of cloth are sewn together and the down is in the middle. Where the seams are stitched, cold air can creep into the bag. The other two methods of sewing a bag are far better, for they provide an even insulation of down everywhere with no cold spots.

When looking at a down bag, or any other, carefully investigate the quality of material and workmanship. Look at the sewing job. Turn the bag inside out and check how the bottom of the bag is made. In a good bag, the sewing job will be good at the foot of the bag as well as everywhere else. Most seams should be hidden.

A good down bag is expensive. It may cost over one hundred dollars. On the other hand, a good down bag should last for ten years or more. An active camper may use a sleeping bag hundreds of times in ten years. So, in buying a sleeping bag, do not balk at the price.

A down sleeping bag is not perfect. As with down clothes, a wet down bag will not insulate you. Also, some people are allergic to down.

This brings us to the Dacron sleeping bag. Dacron is not as warm as down on a per weight basis. It does not pack as well as a down bag. On the other hand, those allergic to down can sleep in a Dacron bag. Also, those headed for wet mountains such as are found in the Pacific Northwest may very well choose a Dacron one.

Almost everything mentioned about a down bag holds true of a Dacron one. However, Dacron comes in battings, which can be slipped into a tube. Baffles are not needed. Also, Dacron does not leak so easily through cloth, so a manufacturer can choose other cloth. These factors, plus the fact that Dacron itself costs less than down initially, make a Dacron bag less expensive than a down one.

Not only are there two types of fillers used in sleeping bags, but there are two different styles of sleeping bags. Some are cut in a rectangular shape. Others are cut and sewn so that they look like Egyptian mummy cases, and, indeed, are called mummy bags.

A rectangular bag can be unzippered in such a way that the bag will lie flat. This is of some advantage at times, for such bags can double as quilts at home. Also, in most cases the zippers are arranged so that two rectangular bags can be put together to form one double bag. The best zippers are not metal ones, for they can catch or break easily. Today, good bags have zippers made of nylon or Delrin. They do not catch so easily. Nylon coil zippers can be fixed by a hiker.

Rectangular bags are preferred by people who summer camp in warmish temperatures. Rectangular bags are rather roomy and you sleep in them more as you do in a regular bed.

Mummy bags cannot be opened up and spread out flat. The mummy bag is warmer and lighter weight than a rectangular bag. Once you are in it, it "hugs" you. There are no air spaces near the body. There is a hood on a mummy bag which can be tightened around the face. When the hood is closed, no drafts can seep down around you. Every time you turn over in a rectangular bag, some air flows into it. Not so with a mummy bag, which, by the way, you can turn over in. Of course, the whole bag goes with you. Thus, the shape of the bag keeps out drafts.

In choosing a bag, get one long enough, especially if you are still growing. If the bag is too long, you will be carrying extra weight, but not much. On the other hand, if it is too short, you will feel cramped and that will interfere with a good night's sleep.

So, what sleeping bag to choose? For cold, dry climates a mummy bag filled with down should certainly be considered. For a backpacking trip where weight is terribly important it would probably be a front runner. For summer camping where it is damp, a rectangular Dacron could

A mummy-type down-filled sleeping bag. (*Courtesy Holubar Mountaineering, Ltd.*)

be the choice. If you can afford it, one of the easiest ways to solve the problem is to get two bags. One could be a down mummy bag and the other either a down or a Dacron rectangular bag. In combination, these can cover a wide range of temperatures and other conditions.

For extremely cold weather, even down to −60°, you can use two bags, one a down mummy rated for 40° inside a rectangular bag rated for −30°. In fact, some people have slept in sleeping bags placed one inside the other in temperatures as low as −100°. Thus, you can find sleeping bags to meet any cold-weather conditions.

When you sleep outdoors, you need some sort of protection under you. Some people use air mattresses, but most today use plastic foam pads. With them you do not have to worry about leaks and the need to pump them up. And the pads are less expensive.

Pads insulate you from the ground. If you sleep on the ground in a sleeping bag, especially in a down one, the body presses the down and it works less well. The pad helps insulate against this heat loss. There are two types—open- and closed-cell. Buy the closed, because it is waterproof and insulates better, but it is firmer and not as soft as the open-cell. Various thicknesses of pad will insulate you differently. For example, ¼ inch will work at about 20°; ⅜ inch at 5°; and ½ inch at −10°. A pad also serves to make you more comfortable. Your bones will not be hitting the ground all night.

In the morning when you wake up, fluff out your sleeping bag. Try to air it out and then pack it in its own separate bag, called a stuff bag.

If you are in camp for a couple of days, air your bag out. Hang it up on a line. Be sure to secure it.

6

Tents

A mountain climber needs a good tent. It should be lightweight, very strong, and windproof. You must be able to tie all doors and vents so that the inside is secure from wind and blowing snow. In this respect, a mountain tent is different from a hiker's tent. It also has more and stronger guy ropes than a hiker's tent. Its general shape is such that it will remain steady in a wind.

There are several varieties of tents to consider. One model is the pyramidical tent. As the name suggests, it has approximately the same shape as an Egyptian pyramid. The roof of the tent is held up by one sturdy pole, which is placed inside the tent in the center of it. The tent has four sides and on each side, except the entrance side, there are usually three guys. On the entrance side there may be either two or three.

The shape of the tent makes it difficult for the wind to hit it and knock it over. The numerous guys hold it against gusts. The steep roof all the way around sheds snow—an important consideration. The shape is one of the oldest and most proven of all.

Most pyramidical tents are designed for four people, but they are a bit crowded with four people actually in them. However, the tents are tall enough so that people can stand up inside. If you are trapped in a tent for several days waiting for a blizzard to stop, you can appreciate how satisfying it is to be able to stand up now and then.

Another commonly used tent is the "mountain tent." This is a two-man tent, and is much smaller than the pyramidical tent. Of course it is lighter weight, too. The tent is often in the shape of a prism; the front and back are triangles. The entrance is usually round. Surrounding it is a tube which can be tied shut with drawstrings. In the upper corners are vents, which can be shut in the same way. The better tents have both front and back entrances—which is helpful for airing out the tent.

In choosing a tent, especially a small one, you must discover whether or not it will sweat excessively. If a tent is made of absolutely waterproof material, it will not only keep water out but keep water inside as well. Plenty of moisture can accumulate inside a tent. Every time you breathe, moisture is given off. If the tent walls are too waterproof, this will accumulate on them. In no time the walls can be dripping with water. You can be miserable in such a tent.

Fortunately, there are two or three ways of keeping moisture out. One is by the use of vents. The other way is to make the tent out of nylon, a material that "breathes." Such a tent will let moisture out, but if not protected it will let moisture in as well. To keep moisture from coming in, the tent needs a fly over it. This is a tentlike roof. All good tents are made so that a fly can be put over them. A problem, however, is that flies often catch the wind and can be blown off. Therefore, many mountain tents today have an inner ceiling of nylon, and over it, with an air space, is another permanent roof which is waterproof. Moisture can thus escape and the upper layers will not blow off.

Where there are no high winds, you can use a fly or get a tent with two roofs. If you are going to camp in very cold weather where there are high winds, you should get a tent which is made of nylon that is wind-resistant but can breathe. Dry, cold snow will blow off the tent, so you will not have to worry about it melting and seeping into the tent. Of course, such a tent can be used only in such conditions. At lower altitudes it will need to be protected by a fly if it is raining.

Another consideration will be the tent poles, which fall into two categories. First, there are simple poles. Some tents are supported inside by one tall pole. Others are supported outside by four poles—two forming a crosslike support at each end of the tent. Simple poles have the advantage that, if they are lost or broken, you can usually make a substitute pole quickly and easily from a tree branch. Many tents today have more elaborate pole arrangements. Often they are of bent aluminum or are in the shape of an upside-down V. If you lose one, it will be difficult to duplicate. On the other hand, some fancy pole arrangements allow a tent to be larger than it ever could be with simple poles.

All tents used in the mountains need a ground cloth. It must be heavier than the rest of the tent, as it takes more abuse. Most mountain tents have a hole in the ground cloth, which you can open and shut with a zipper. It is meant for cooking in emergencies.

In choosing a tent, see to it that the doorways, vents, and so on can be closed with drawstrings. Zippers are good, but ice can form on them, so have an alternate, foolproof way of closing up the tent.

Perhaps the tent's fabric material is the most important consideration. It must be strong enough to take high winds, one of the greatest dangers to a mountain climber. Even the strongest tents have occasionally been ripped to ribbons in winds, as winds of over a hundred miles an hour are not uncommon in mountains. If you

A mountain tent for two. (*Courtesy Holubar Mountaineering, Ltd.*)

are planning a trip to places known to have high winds, which include almost all areas above timberline, be certain that the tent is built for it. Pound for pound the sturdiest material is nylon. The mountain climber can ignore other materials. The best is rip-stop nylon. Of course, the heavier the material is, the stronger it will be. Nylon is rated in ounces of material per square yard; so when you see a tent listed as made of 1.9-ounce rip-stop nylon, it means that the nylon weighs 1.9 ounces a square yard.

Nylon, however tightly woven, is not windproof enough by itself. Today nylon tents are coated with polymers, usually urethane or superurethane. They make the material more windproof and somewhat water-resistant. Do not get a tent coated with rubber, as it can crack in cold weather.

When considering a tent, pay close attention to the workmanship that went into it. See that all the seams are straight and that there is no sloppiness along them. Places of greatest wear, such as where the poles fit into or against the cloth, should be reinforced, as well as places where there are guy ropes attached. Try to find out how many stitches per inch there are in the tent. The more the better. Zippers should be made of nylon, since in cold weather it doesn't freeze as fast as metal.

A good tent should have mosquito netting. Though at times mountain climbers may be free of these pests, there are times when they can be a major problem.

Good tents are expensive, but do not stint on one. For a mountain climber, a tent is a lifesaving piece of equipment. In a tent you can survive howling winds and subzero temperatures.

It is difficult to put up a tent in a high wind, and you must be careful how you do it. When the tent is unwrapped, take one of the end guy lines and secure it. Really secure it, so there is no possibility the tent will suddenly fly off into the next county. Arrange the tent so that the wind will blow along its length. Peg down the windward side first. If the tent is flapping too much, have your companion try to hold it down while you get in the pegs and secure the tent. Do not worry too much at first about getting the pegs in just so. After the tent is up, it is easier to go back over the work and get everything in shape. Try to keep the tent low until the last minute so that it does not balloon up.

A tent presents a fire hazard. Whenever possible, cook away from it, downwind from it. Only during a howling blizzard would you actually use a stove in a tent. Even then, you should consider whether it is worth it. Of course, you should not smoke in a tent.

If you are ever in a snowstorm and the tent gets plastered with snow, be very sure not to use a stove. At times snow can seal a tent until it is airproof. A stove in a small tent with no oxygen to spare can quickly use it all up.

Keep heavy snows off your tent. Some mountain climbers carry along lightweight aluminum shovels to clean away snow. Really heavy snow may collapse a tent, and shut off the air.

Before entering a tent, try to brush snow off your clothing as much as possible. Any and all snow brought in will eventually puddle on the floor in pools of icy-cold water.

Be careful of your equipment around the tent. The points of ice axes and crampons will easily put holes in it. So will other metal objects.

Take along some nylon repair tape to patch any small holes. Since tents get dirty very easily, it might be worth it to take along a small, lightweight whisk broom. No matter how careful one is, in a few days a tent will have dust and sand in it.

7

Cooking Equipment

In choosing any cooking equipment, look for items which are lightweight, strong, and reliable.

There is a wide variety of camping stoves. Only a few, though, are of interest to a mountain climber.

Let us first consider those stoves powered by butane and propane. Butane is not used in very cold weather, as it freezes at 15° F. It is difficult to get going properly unless the temperature is well above freezing. For summer use, however, you might choose a butane stove. They operate from metal bottles of gas, are quite simple to use, and are safer than gasoline or kerosene stoves. They do have a drawback. When the bottles are half full, they don't throw out much heat. Another distinct drawback is the fact that they put out less heat than either gasoline or kerosene stoves.

Propane stoves are almost identical to butane stoves but have the advantage that they can be used in cold weather.

You might consider an alcohol stove for a short trip. Alcohol itself is not as powerful or as lightweight as gasoline and kerosene, but the stove is lighter. An added advantage is that it is easy to operate.

On a long trip it might be best to take along a gasoline or kerosene stove. The lighter weight of the fuel offsets the weight of the stove.

Gasoline stoves operate on white gas, which means gasoline with no lead in it. It burns with a hot, steady flame. Some gasoline stoves need to be pumped to get pressure up. In others the flame raises the heat of the gasoline so that it vaporizes and burns. A pump adds

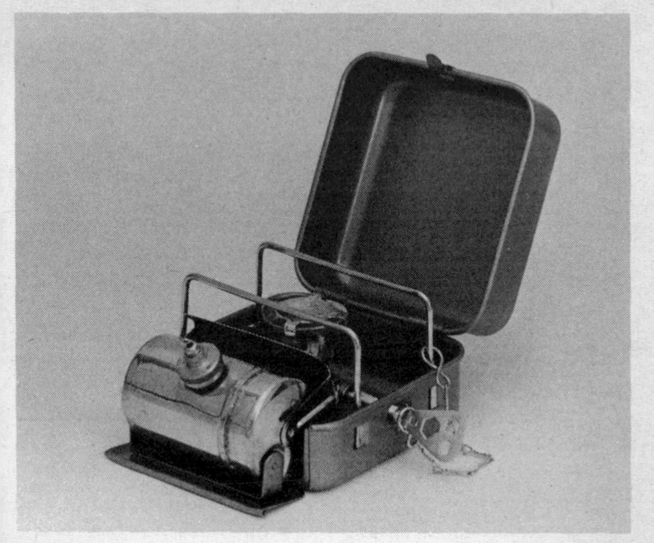

A compact stove, fueled by white gas. Such a stove is only five by five by three inches and weighs 1¾ pounds. (*Courtesy Recreational Equipment, Inc.*)

weight and calls for more bother, but it increases the power and heat of the flame considerably.

A kerosene stove is very much like a gasoline stove, but don't try to switch fuels. That would be extremely dangerous. While it may be difficult to find white gas in foreign countries, kerosene can usually be obtained easily. Both gasoline and kerosene are easily obtainable in the United States.

Now let us look at the pros and cons of the various stoves. The butane and propane are by far the easiest to use, but they weigh the most and do not give off as much heat. Of the liquid-fuel stoves, the alcohol one is the easiest to use and the lightest, but the fuel does not give off as much heat per pound as gasoline and kerosene. Gasoline has a distinct drawback. It can explode. Also, spilled gasoline is far more likely to burst into flame than kerosene. Kerosene will never explode.

Kerosene, however, is dirtier. If gasoline spills, it will eventually evaporate and leave almost no odor. Spilled kerosene does not evaporate and it leaves an odor for a long time. Worse, the smoky kerosene flame can taint food a bit.

A note of caution: When you buy a stove, read the directions thoroughly and carefully. Try it out in a safe place long before you go on a trip. Do not use your stove in a tent, unless you are trapped by a blizzard. Even then, it is best to try to survive on cold foods. Never use a stove to heat up your tent.

To carry gasoline, kerosene, or alcohol, you will need a metal bottle. Be sure to get the correct bottle for the fuel used. Some can hold alcohol, for example, and some cannot.

It is handy to have a funnel for pouring the fuel into a stove.

If the stove calls for primer, it, too, has to be taken along. A small eyedropper is usually used to place it properly in the stove.

On a mountain climbing trip you need only a few eating utensils.

You will need a drinking cup. Often it is carried outside, either on a pack or on your belt. You want a rugged cup made of metal or tough plastic. The handles of metal cups, however, often become too hot to hold when they contain hot liquids. A Sierra cup is a metal cup with a heavy wire handle which never becomes that hot. It is a popular cup for campers. Plastic cups with plastic handles are good, as their handles don't conduct heat.

You will need a pot for cooking. It should be of a size and shape to fit your stove. It should fit exactly over the flame and should have a wire handle so that it can be lifted from the flame with a stick. Having two pots is often convenient. Aluminum pots and pans are lightweight and strong.

You will not need plates, as you will eat out of pots, pans, and sometimes, cups. You will, however, need a spoon. A tablespoon of stainless steel is usually the best. You rarely need a fork. Some people use jackknives for cooking and eating purposes, but I don't think much of the idea, for food can gum them up. Jackknives are difficult to clean properly, they can be dangerous, and they can cut through plastic containers too easily. It is best to carry a regular table knife for food. Take one that can cut bread and cheese and that is easy to clean.

Most canteens are made of either metal or plastic. In buying a canteen, get one which carries a quart of water. The screw top should have some sort of arrangement, such as a chain, which will keep it from getting lost. Be sure that the top is easy to work, as handling a canteen and its top with bulky mittens on can be difficult. In very cold weather you do not want to be forced to take off your mittens to handle a cold metal top.

Mountain climbers have some problem with keeping water in a canteen from freezing. A quart of warm water will take a long time to freeze, even in sub-zero weather. I cannot recall one freezing solid, though slush will often form. Nevertheless, some other precautions can be taken. One is to keep a canteen where it will be protected from cold wind. Place it in a pack, where it is easy to get. Some climbers carry lemonade, slightly sweetened with sugar. This is a tasty drink, and the acid and sugar together lower the freezing point. Of course, lemonade cannot be carried in a metal canteen as the acid will react with it.

Some people recommend placing a canteen in a sleeping bag at night to keep it warm and from freezing. But why should you buy an expensive sleeping bag which is designed to keep you warm and then place in it a canteen of water which will cool you down? It is better to pour warm water into a canteen just before "sacking out" for the night and place it inside a pack surrounded by insulation in the form of sweaters, down jackets, and so on. Protected like that, it will not freeze except under the most severe conditions.

Finding pure, clean water can sometimes be a problem. At the beginning of a trip it is no problem, for you can bring some water with you. Beyond that point you have to be careful.

Unless you know for sure that water is safe, you should boil it before using it. At elevations below 9,000 feet you can boil it for about twenty minutes and it will then be safe. Above the elevation you have to boil the water longer, or use halazone tablets.

Since mountain climbers are frequently in regions

which are uninhabited, they can usually find good sources of water. There are a couple of ways of finding it. Water pouring off a large snow bank is safe, if you know that no one has contaminated it. If you are in an area where you can see the watershed for a given stream and you know that no one has been there, you can trust the stream. Of course, snow itself is pure and, when melted down, makes good drinking water.

Snow, strange as it may seem, is somewhat difficult to melt down. It always takes more heat than expected. Stirring will help make it melt faster. Once the snow is melted, the water from it often tastes blah. It is worth making tea or lemonade or something to give the water some taste.

Springs are usually not to be used as it is very difficult to tell where the water came from. Do not use water from a large stream or river as, again, you have no idea where it came from or who was near it.

Be sure always to have enough water with you. High winds can dehydrate you quickly, especially in the mountains where the cold air can be remarkably dry. It is believed that several climbers have died of dehydration rather than exposure. Furthermore, if your system does not have enough water, you tire out much more easily.

8

Food

My views about food are rather unorthodox. However, I will try to give you my opinions based on my own personal experience.

First of all, mountain climbers use concentrated foods, such as dried foods or oils. Any food which is partly liquid is too heavy to carry. Once you have planned a trip, take along about 2¼ pounds per person per day of the most concentrated foods available. It is the amount of food which you can carry that dictates the length of time you can be in the mountains away from civilization. Few people can carry over fifty pounds of food, plus all of their other needs, so that it is very difficult indeed for anyone to stay out in the wilds more than three weeks. Of course, 2¼ pounds of food is somewhat of a minimum for people engaged in extremely strenuous activity.

When planning a trip, think of food as being in various categories. First, there are the fats. Per pound they contain more calories than any other food. At home you do not normally eat so much fat, but on a long hiking trip fats give you a great deal of physical energy. The body burns them slowly—thus, they go a long way. This is why it is better to eat fats in the morning. There are several fatty foods: butter, some cheeses, oily nuts, and so on.

Next, a hiker needs carbohydrates—that is, sugars and starches. There are starches such as bread, dry cereals, melba toast, crackers, and so on. Sugar is important, especially since the body can absorb it quickly and effectively. So take along sugar itself, candies, and so on. People suffering from the cold respond to condensed milk, which is a canned sugary milk.

Proteins are, as the food books say, the building blocks of the body. Consider nuts, peanuts, cheese, powdered milk, and so on.

Drinks are important. Some powdered teas mix directly with cold water and are thus more convenient than instant coffee. Cocoa and milk can be mixed. Acid drinks such as lemonade are always welcome. You can get lemonade powder which can be mixed with water.

Dried fruits are a must. Since constipation is a common complaint, figs, prunes, and so on can be eaten. Carry along some vitamin pills, especially if you are camping for over a week.

Once you consider your food needs in terms of the types of food you should have, then you can plan your meals so that each day you will have fat, sugar, protein, and vitamins. A balanced diet helps the digestion, and your body can use everything more effectively.

Freeze-dried foods today come in many varieties and are easy to prepare. They have many advantages: You can get prepared meals; they are quickly cooked; they are nonperishable and lightweight. They also have disadvantages: Only special camping stores carry them, and they are expensive.

I see no reason why a mountain climber cannot plan a meal so that everything can be bought in a supermarket. This has a great advantage. Many times, on the spur of the moment, I have decided to go camping while in a small town. By simply going to the nearest supermarket, I could get all I needed.

Let us consider some menus. First of all, we can start with a no-muss, no-fuss menu for a five-day trip, wherein you never make a fire and never see a dirty dish. The following menu will give you an idea of what can be taken.

For five days take along:

1. Cheese. This is the mainstay of the diet. It provides protein, and some fat. Get cheese which is easy to digest. I have found that Velveeta is quite easy to eat, and it does not bother me as a much more expensive "strong" cheese might do. But any mild cheese which will keep should be all right. Take two or three types.

2. Raisins. They are an old standby. Unlike other dried fruit, they can be eaten along the trail as a snack.

3. Dried fruit. There is a wide selection: apples, pears, apricots, dates, and so on. With most, it is best to soak them overnight and let them swell, then eat them.

4. Bread, crackers, melba toast, etc. Rye bread holds up and does not dry out as white bread will. On day trips I sometimes take canned Boston brown bread. I have found that melba toast works quite well, though it is bulky. Crackers should be good, but I never take them as I feel they will break up. Dried cereal such as Familia is also good.

5. Butter. Butter is really great. Smear it on everything. Of all foods, it provides the most calories per weight. A few people may want to substitute margarine for butter.

6. Chocolate bars. Chocolate is an old standby. It has given an extra boost to many Arctic explorers and mountain climbers. Other candies are not good substitutes; chocolate is a stimulant and contains some caffeine and some theobroma, which is a milder stimulant, both of which seem to be absolutely safe. Between the stimulant and the sugar—and that marvelous taste (theobroma, by the way, means "food of the gods")—chocolate is unbeatable.

7. Nuts and peanuts. Peanuts are not really nuts, but in food value they are close enough. Nuts provide needed protein and have some starch. Peanuts and nuts are good for snacks.

8. Powdered milk. Powdered milk mixes easily with cold water. It provides more protein. Some cocoa can be taken to mix in with it too. A little bit of sugar makes powdered milk taste more like the real thing.

9. Sugar. Sugar is needed but, of course, it must be mixed or sprinkled on things. Mix some with milk, tea, etc. Sprinkle it on dried fruit. I have even put it on cheese. Sugar does give you quick energy and of all foods digests the fastest.

10. Tea. Powdered tea will mix with cold water. Get the instant type. You may be forced to melt snow, and tea knocks out the poor taste of it.

11. Salt. A mountain climber needs salt. The exercise will make you sweat, and sweat takes salt out of the body. It needs to be replaced. If too much is lost, you need salt tablets, but otherwise you simply need salt on your food.

12. Dessert. Fig Newtons, date bars, and so on are good desserts.

13. Acid. Since this diet lacks vegetables and fresh fruits, you must make a substitute. Tang and other dehydrated drink mixes have citric acid in them. You need some acids to balance your diet.

14. A can of condensed milk. This is an emergency drink for someone suffering from the cold. If you are on a summer trip in a warm region, forget it.

15. Salami. Hard salami, such as pepperoni, will stay fresh for two or three days, especially if you are hiking in a cold climate. Use it as you would cheese.

Let us now consider a longer trip. You will need to do some cooking and have some hot meals. You immediately increase the number of things you will eat. Add to the basic five-day diet the following:

1. Cookable starches. Take along some instant rice, instant cereals, instant mashed potatoes, and so on. Below about 12,000 feet you can take those things which cook for thirty minutes, but above that elevation some things simply do not seem to cook. Instant rice and mashed potatoes will cook easily at high altitudes. But I recall once cooking some noodles for a good hour and they still were inedible. The boiling water never got hot enough.

2. Soups. It is strange how soup makes such a world of difference. It helps settle one's stomach. Moreover, there is such a wide variety of flavors available in dehydrated soups that you can always find some goody. Some soups, if made thick enough, can act as sauces for other foods, such as mashed potatoes.

3. Dried beef. This is not as easy to find as most items. It never serves as a major item, as it is a far cry from steak.

4. Bacon. I've always been of two minds about bacon. In one way it is a great breakfast food, being fatty. However, once you have eaten it, you are immediately faced with a greasy pan which must be carefully cleaned. Believe me, a greasy pan without good hot water and steel wool is very much harder to clean than a pot that has had cereal in it. Secondly, bacon melts in hot weather; so it *must* be kept in an oilproof container. Butter, which

is also oily, is far easier to pack. I took bacon once and never will again.

5. Eggs. You can get decent dehydrated scrambled eggs. Eggs are one of the very few foods which supply all needed proteins.

6. Vegetables. Dried vegetables are best obtained from a camper's supply house. The freeze-dried are the best.

7. Spices. I have never taken any; but they are so light in weight—next to nothing—and can make such a difference in the way food tastes that they would be a great idea, and next time I go on a long trip I'll try some. Pepper comes to mind first, but is the one I use least. A good cookbook would give you all sorts of ideas.

8. Jell-O. I have often taken Jell-O in places where I am sure that there will be some snow near camp, which has meant most of the time. Jell-O is good because you can easily make it the last thing at night and place it in a snow bank all night. In the morning you have a pot of Jell-O.

9. Vitamin pills. Why not? Just do not overdo it.

You will notice that the above foods are rather quick and easy to prepare, which is as it should be. You can forget about taking flour, baking powder, and so on, as the old-timers did. On the other hand, you can go camping with even simpler foods to prepare. All you have to do is go to a big, well-stocked camping store and get freeze-dried foods. You can get all sorts of interesting, quick, no-fuss, no-muss items. I would recommend it, except that they are so expensive.

Now that we have our general food list, let us think about the individual meals. Mountain climbers usually cook only two hot meals a day—breakfast and supper. Lunch is usually cold, as the climbers are on the move around noontime. They frequently have a midmorning snack and an afternoon snack. The midmorning snack is especially important, for climbers may start off at 4:00 A.M. and not stop for lunch until noon. That is a stretch of eight hours. The midafternoon snack is important, too, for at that time people are often tired, and the snack gives them a needed lift.

The following lists will give you some suggestions for menus.

BREAKFAST. Powdered milk, dry or cooked cereal, hot tea, sugar, dried fruits which have been soaked overnight. It is best to eat fats in the morning, so bread with a lot of butter on it would be a good idea. If you bring bacon, it should be used at breakfast time. Eggs have quite a good deal of fat in them, and they, too, are best at breakfast. Eat a good hearty breakfast, but don't overdo it, as you will start hiking immediately afterwards.

MIDMORNING SNACK. Powdered milk and tea, which mix with cold water, are good. You could also have dry cereal, crackers, cookies, or melba toast with butter. "Gorp"—a mixture of chocolates, raisins, and peanuts—is a favorite snack for many climbers. A citrus-fruit drink is often delicious with your snack. If you are really hungry, date rolls or Fig Newtons or something similar are good to have.

LUNCH. Most hikers will eat a cold lunch prepared in advance. Cheese and bread or crackers often make up the backbone of a good lunch. You can vary it with salami or other meat for a sandwich. Raisins are good. If you have the time to set up a stove, you should probably make up a pot of hot soup and also have some tea. Many climbers like to end lunch with a candy bar or other sweet food.

MIDAFTERNOON SNACK. By midafternoon, climbers are often beginning to feel the wear of a long day. This is especially true if they woke up before dawn. The midafternoon snack can help pull you together. It is usually a repeat of the morning snack.

SUPPER. Supper is the big meal on almost any mountain climbing trip. By the time supper rolls around, camp is made and you have some time to spend preparing a meal. More to the point, perhaps, is that it is the one meal at which you can really relax. It is often the time when people can carry on conversations. Last but not least, it is the time for sitting around a campfire.

Most suppers begin with hot soup, sometimes thickened with eggs. The main course is often a noodle, rice, or mashed potato dish. You can easily add gravy, vegetables, cheese, dried beef, or the like to any of these dishes. Each night you can vary the mixtures as well as adding spices, Bac-o-bits, etc.

For vegetables you can have either dehydrated vegetables or vegetable soup.

Cups of hot chocolate and a few sweets help top off a good meal. Hot drinks are especially good, as the nights in mountainous areas are usually cool or cold.

HOW TO PLAN MEALS. So far there have been only general suggestions for meals. Next, we should see how individual meals are planned. The following meals will only be samples, as actual meals will vary a great deal.

First, be sure to plan carefully all meals long before you ever hit the trail. This can cut down on errors. You have to be sure *before* getting on the trail that you have enough food. It would be a serious mistake to end up with too little. Another mistake would be to carry too much food, or to remember lunches and forget breakfasts. Furthermore, by careful planning you can be sure that you have enough variety.

How do you plan? The best way, if you have no previous experience, is to start thinking about a trip a couple of weeks before going on it. Buy all the food planned for the trip, and prepare and cook it all with the stove you will take, as if you were on the trail. Eat nothing else during that time. Afterwards you will pretty much know what went wrong. This procedure will give you experience before you ever go on a trip. Thus you can become an "expert camp cook" without ever having been on a trail.

The next best way for an inexperienced person to plan food for a camping trip is to make a careful list. First, write down each meal. Next, you know that you need 2¼ pounds of concentrated food per day, so you divide this amount into separate meals. You may decide to eat ten ounces of food for breakfast, five ounces for the midmorning snack, six ounces for lunch, five ounces for the midafternoon snack, and ten ounces for supper. This will give you a total of thirty-six ounces (2¼ pounds) correctly divided up into a reasonable scheme. It might sound like slim pickings at first, but don't forget that most of the dried food will bulk out to two or three times its weight when it absorbs water.

Next, multiply the daily meals by the number of days out. Thus, if you are going to spend five days on the trail, you will need fifty ounces, or three pounds two ounces of various foods for breakfast—powdered milk, cereals, dried fruits, and so on, according to the menu you set up. It is easiest to buy each meal that way.

Before leaving for a trip, arrange all the food you have bought on a table. Separate the meals and snacks for each day. In this way you can check all the food to see what might be missing or if you have too much of anything. This procedure is especially important for long trips. If you go for a trip lasting more than five days, you should check, check, and check again your food supplies.

From your very first trip on, it is wise to list all the food you carry. Write down every single item, its weight, whether or not you enjoyed it, and if you thought you carried too much of it or too little. Also, list those items that you wish you had taken with you. After a while, such lists become invaluable. After a few trips you can refine your food list to suit your needs.

A SAMPLE MENU

If you are going camping for the first time and have not had time enough to develop your own food list and experiment with it, you can try the following menu.

First day	Second day	Third day
	Breakfast	
dry cereal, 4 oz.	granola, 4 oz.	cooked cereal—instant Cream of Wheat, oatmeal, etc., 4 oz.
dried fruit, 2 oz.	dried fruit, 2 oz.	dried fruit, 1 oz.
powdered milk, 2 oz.	powdered milk, 2 oz.	powdered milk, 2 oz.
sugar, 1½ oz.	sugar, 1½ oz.	fruit drink mix, 1 oz.
tea mix, ¼ oz.	tea mix, ¼ oz.	sugar, 1 oz.
		tea mix, ¼ oz.
	Midmorning snack	
raisins, 2 oz.	cookies, 2 oz.	granola, 2 oz.
chocolate, 2 oz.	dates, 2 oz.	energy bar, 2 oz.
tea mix, ¼ oz.	tea mix, ¼ oz.	tea mix, ¼ oz.
powdered milk, 1 oz.	powdered milk, 1 oz.	powdered milk, 1 oz.
	Lunch	
cheese, 2 oz.	cheese, 2 oz.	cheese, 2 oz.
butter, 1 oz.	peanut butter, 2 oz.	butter, 1 oz.
bread, 1 oz.	bread or crackers, 1 oz.	bread, 1 oz.
nuts, 2 oz.		nuts, 1 oz.

First day	Second day	Third day
tea mix, ¼ oz.	chocolate, 1 oz. tea mix, ¼ oz.	chocolate, 1 oz. tea mix, ¼ oz.
	Midafternoon snack	
gorp, 4 oz. tea mix, ¼ oz. powdered milk, 1 oz.	chocolate, 2 oz. energy bar, 2 oz. tea mix, ¼ oz. powdered milk, 1 oz.	gorp, 4 oz. tea mix, ¼ oz. powdered milk, 1 oz.
	Supper	
rice, 3 oz. pea soup, 1 oz. cheese, 3 oz. dried tomatoes, ¼ oz. butter, 1 oz. powdered milk, 1 oz. tea mix, ¼ oz. sugar, ¼ oz. spices, negligible vitamin pill	noodles, 3 oz. vegetable soup, 1 oz. beef jerky, 3 oz. butter, ¾ oz. chocolate, powdered milk, and sugar mixed, 1 oz. tea mix, ¼ oz. spices, negligible vitamin pill	instant mashed potatoes, 3 oz. beef gravy, ½ oz. tomato soup, 1 oz. beef jerky, 3 oz. butter, 1 oz. chocolate, powdered milk, and sugar mixed, 1 oz. tea mix, ¼ oz. spices, negligible vitamin pill
	Totals	
36¼ oz.	35½ oz.	35¾ oz.

Before we close our discussion of menus, we must cover one more topic. Sometimes mountain climbers suffer at high altitudes from a real loss of appetite. Though their bodies desperately need food, their stomachs balk. To stimulate the appetite these climbers need something which will interest them. There is such a variety of freeze-dried foods that there is bound to be something—shrimp, "ice cream," Mexican dinners, you name it—that is appetizing. Fortunately, lack of hunger is not a common experience and only happens at high altitudes; most of the time the opposite is true—people wolf anything down.

It is usually better to take off the store wrappings before you pack foods. Most of the time they weigh too much and rip easily. For example, dried cereal usually comes in a cardboard box. A nylon bag is lighter and it won't burst. Nuts sometimes come in tough plastic bags, but once they are opened, nothing will hold them; so they need to be put into a nylon bag.

Nylon bags have drawstrings to close them. Tough

plastic bags are closed by twisting the necks and securing them with rubber bands.

All oily foods, such as butter, are placed in plastic containers with square oilproof covers and secured with rubber bands or screw tops. Butter "eats" rubber, so be sure never to use a container with rubber gaskets.

Many powdered things are best kept in plastic bottles. When they are needed, just pour them out. This is much better than fooling around with a bag.

Get a salt shaker. Many have a side for pepper. Such a shaker adds almost no weight, and is better than trying to control the amount of salt poured on food. A "dump" of salt can ruin something.

Sometimes it is easier to premix things. For example, premixing tea and sugar, if that is the way you like it, is easier than unscrewing a bottle of tea, pouring it in a cup of water, screwing the top back on, and then getting the sugar bottle and going through it all again.

During a trip keep all the food together in one part of your pack. Do not have it scattered all over the place.

Today you can be a mountain climber and never make a campfire. Most cooking is done on stoves. Also, some areas prohibit fires.

When camping, see if you need a fire permit. Rangers or police can inform you.

Of course, everyone should know how to make a campfire. Choose a good place for the fire. Build it on bare ground. Clean away all leaves and anything flammable. See which way the wind is blowing and consider where sparks may fly. Do not start a fire too close to your tent.

It is usually best to make a fire in a little "fireplace" made of a crescent-shaped grouping of stones. See to it that the wind enters from the open side.

To build the fire, first gather some dry wood. Get some small pieces, twigs of about matchstick size, then some about pencil size. Follow that up with some from about an inch thick to about three inches thick. With the latter you do not have to be exact of course. Have everything in one place *before* you build the fire. Many fires have started well but then died down. Then the camper went to look for wood, only to come back to a dead fire. And so he had to start all over again.

Take some match-sized twigs and place them carefully into the form of a tiny tepee. Above that build a larger tepee of pencil-sized twigs. Or, if you like log cabins better, you can build around the inner tepee a little log cabin of pencil-sized twigs. Many campers pride themselves on using just one match to set this thing going. It does save matches. Light the match near the tepee, but do not stick it in immediately; let the wooden or paper shaft of the match catch on fire first. Then slowly thrust it into the tepee. In a few seconds there should be a nice blaze. If so, be ready to build more log cabins with wood of increasing thicknesses. Once they have burned down and you have a hot enough fire, place two large pieces of wood on it and one supported by them, with plenty of air space. Air space is the key to the whole thing. The more air space you have, the hotter and faster the flames will be.

Note that no paper was used in the fire-making process. Strange as it may seem, paper is not very good for making fires, as the ashes do not break down rapidly and begin to clog the fire and shut off air.

What happens if it is raining? Look for dead trees which still have bark on them. Peel off the bark. The wood underneath should be dry. If it is pouring, work under a poncho or in a tent, but be very careful you do not cut the tent. Keep your new fuel dry. If possible, find an aspen or birch tree. Birch bark sheds so much water that even "wet" bark burns. If all this does not work, find a dry rotting log. The inside should be dry. Watch out for the insects that might be in it, or snakes under it.

If you are hiking along on a nice sunny day and you see that by nightfall it will be raining, it would not hurt to collect at least some dry kindling beforehand, even if it is extra weight.

Snow is a more difficult problem than rain. If you are camping in snow, dig down to the ground for a place to build a fire and see that it will not melt snow down into it. Often, however, it is easier to construct a platform on top of the snow. In deep snow you must do this. Make a "raft" of wood. If available, place flat stones or dirt on top of it. If not, seal it with more wood. Once the platform is made, build the fire on it.

Gathering wood in deep snow or old snow can be

difficult. Wood which has been in snow will get wet all the way through and stay wet for weeks afterward. It may even look dry on the outside. The trick is to find wood which has not been under the snow. The only place, therefore, is above any snow line. Twigs on a dead tree high up, almost out of reach will almost always be dry. The higher the better, for wind and sunlight will have helped dry them out.

If you are going to use a campfire for cooking, be sure to arrange the stones properly. Support your pot and/or pan from green sticks. Some people use grills. I find them a nuisance. I bought one once and several times it collapsed, spilling things. I can never recall my stones falling or a pot spilling on them. Secondly, the grill was virtually impossible to clean. The mixture of soot and fat will not come off. After those experiences I threw mine away. Anyway, who wants to carry the weight?

Small campfires are far easier to cook over and manage than big ones. Big fires occasionally have a place, though. Sometimes it is nice to make a good one and just sit around it.

A warning: Sometimes people find they are carrying too much food and leave some of it near a trail for others. This is dangerous. Such foods can rot or even become poisonous. Never leave food like that. Carry it out. Never eat foods you may find on a trail or in the mountains.

9

Mountain Climbing Equipment

Mountain climbers need to use specialized equipment to climb steep cliffs and icy slopes. The equipment has to be well chosen. Go only to the best stores recommended by local mountain clubs.

The rope you use to climb a mountain or a cliff is of the greatest importance. Your life may very well depend upon it.

The first requirement of a rope is that it be absolutely reliable. When you go climbing you should be sure that the rope is in perfect condition, that it is not more than one year old, and that no one has fallen on it or placed a great weight on it. If you have any reason to question a rope, throw it away.

The mountain climbing rope must be strong. The materials in a rope have a great deal to do with how strong it will be. Ropes can be made of many types of fibers: hemp, manila, sisal, cotton, nylon, Dacron, steel, and many more. The strengths of various fibers vary a great deal. For example, a half-inch rope made of sisal will support about 2,120 pounds, whereas a half-inch rope made of nylon will support a weight of 7,100 pounds. Mountain climbing ropes are usually made of nylon because it is so strong. Few ropes are stronger than nylon. Steel is stronger, but it is impractical to use.

Another asset of nylon is that it stretches when a weight is suddenly put on it. If you fall, the rope will "give" rather than jolt you, thus avoiding possible injuries. Nylon rope, unlike some other types, does not mildew. It sheds ice crystals quite well. Water does not affect it. Furthermore, nylon rope feels good in your hand. The fibers in steel rope, for example, could easily cut your hands to ribbons.

Nylon rope is not perfect, however. Chemicals can deteriorate it. For example, paint fumes can react with it and badly weaken it. Never store a nylon rope in a janitor's closet or workshop areas where cleaning chemicals, paint fumes, etc., can be near it. Always store a nylon rope in a cool place.

Nylon rope can melt at around 450° F. Frictional heat can sometimes reach this temperature. Nylon rope should never be used where one rope slides over another. Some slings of nylon rope, through which another rope was passed, have been known to melt and break.

There are two types of nylon rope on the market for mountain climbers. All nylon ropes are made of thousands of separate fibers. A hawser rope is one in which the fibers are twisted into strands and the strands in turn twisted into rope. Most ropes are hawser ropes. The other way of making a rope is to leave all the strands straight and parallel. It is obvious that in such a rope the strands would all separate. To keep them in place, the strands are covered with a sheath of woven nylon material. Such a rope is called a kernmantle rope.

Both ropes have advantages and disadvantages. Kernmantle rope for any given diameter is slightly stronger than hawser rope. A kernmantle rope of 7/16-inch diameter has a breaking strength of 5,900 pounds, whereas a hawser rope of the same diameter has a breaking strength of 5,500 pounds. Kernmantle is easier in some ways to handle, for it twists less than hawser rope. It does not stretch as much as hawser rope, but enough not to jolt a climber too much.

It would seem that kernmantle would win hands down as the choice of rope to get. Unfortunately this is not the case, for kernmantle rope has a serious defect. It does not hold knots as well as hawser rope. An expert climber can probably always get the right knots tied in it, but a beginner could have real trouble. Since a rope is only as strong as the knots in it, I do not recommend that a beginner use a kernmantle rope.

A hawser rope has another advantage. You can check its fibers to see if they are frayed, whereas kernmantle fibers are hidden.

The larger the diameter of a given rope, the stronger

it is. Many tests have been run on ropes to determine what size is the best for a mountain climbing rope. Most people use a rope 7/16 inch in diameter. If you are buying a foreign-made rope, the rope should be 11 millimeters in diameter or larger. 11 mm = 0.4331 inch or almost exactly 7/16 inch. One hundred feet of 7/16-inch nylon rope weighs about 5½ pounds.

Rock climbers climb together in groups of two or three on a single rope. The length can vary from 100 to 150 feet. When two people climb together, they usually use a rope about 120 feet in length.

If you plan to be crossing glaciers, then a nylon hawser rope of an inch in diameter is best. As we will see later on, glacier rescues are done with prusik knots, which are best made with the thicker rope, for an inch-thick nylon rope does not stretch as much as one 7/16 inch. It should be about the same length as a rock climbing rope.

For rappelling you can use a lighter-weight nylon rope ¼ inch in diameter. It will hold about 1,850 pounds. Some rappel ropes are six hundred feet long.

For a waist band obtain hemp rope about ¾ inch in diameter. Get it about twenty-five feet long so that it can go around your waist seven times. The rope is used for fastening on the nylon climbing rope. Hemp is used as it will not melt from frictional heat.

Nylon rope lasts about a year if there has been no fall on it and there is no excessive fraying. At the end of a year you will need to buy new rope. It is a shame that a rather expensive item has such a short life span. But it is better that the rope has a short life span rather than the climber. When throwing away a rope, be sure either to cut it into small pieces or to burn it so no one accidentally uses it.

When not in use, ropes are kept in neat loops. Make them about two feet in diameter. As you loop the rope, be careful to see that there are no kinks in it and that it is not twisted. Each loop should be the same size. Secure them as shown in the chapter on knots. Loops of climbing rope are usually carried over the shoulder with the opposite arm through the loops.

In using the rope, be sure never to step on it nor let any sharp object hit it. It should not be used on rocks in such a way that it will be pulled over sharp edges of

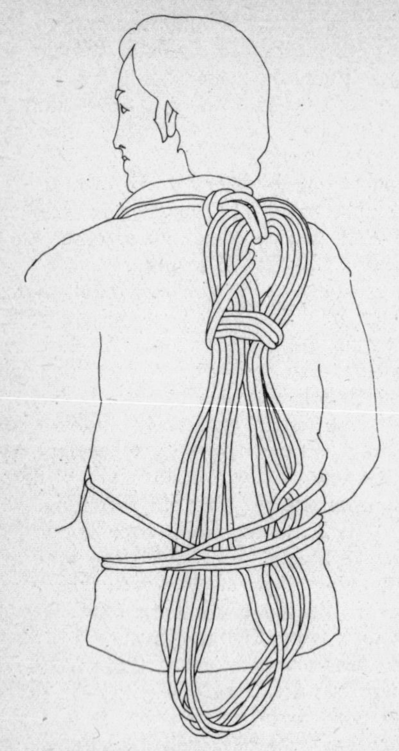

The proper way to carry a rope.

rock. Of course, the rope will fray a little bit in use, but you must use common sense to see that any and all wear and tear on the rope is kept to a minimum.

When two people are roped together and walking along, the excess rope is coiled and held in the hands. Long lengths of rope are not dragged on the ground or over snow. The length of rope between the people should be off the ground. The only possible exception is when you are probing for crevasses on a glacier.

In any climbing operations, see to it that there are no dangerous loops or coils made in the rope, as that will cause trouble. A loop of rope can catch a climber's feet and throw him if the rope is being quickly pulled by a falling person. A loop of rope can kink up and catch in a carabiner as the rope moves through it. We'll have more to say about that later, but it is all part of tending the rope properly.

At all times watch or listen for falling rocks. One may hit a rope. If that happens, immediately check the rope to see if any damage has occurred.

All beginners should practice with experienced climbers for several weekends in a row to get the idea of how to tend a rope. It is not difficult, but it takes a little bit of doing to get the knack of it.

Pitons (pronounced "pee-tons") are specially made metal pegs used in rock climbing. You pound them into cracks in rocks, and they are made to jam tightly in the crack. Most of them have metal arches or V-shaped sides which bend and hold in a crack. A well-placed piton can hold over 10,000 pounds. Thus, it can offer a secure place for the climber to "tie into" the mountainside.

So many people have mistaken ideas of how pitons are used that it might be best to get rid of false ideas first. One does not pound pitons in and climb up them hand over hand. A climbing rope is never attached directly to a piton, in spite of the fact that there is a hole large enough in it to pass a rope through it.

The piton is placed in a rock crack and a carabiner, which is something like a snap link, is attached to it. The rope goes through the carabiner.

There are several types of pitons made to fit different sized cracks. Obviously some cracks are very thin and some very wide.

For a narrow crack, climbers use a leaf piton. It has a blade which looks something like a knife blade. At one end is a flat surface which can be hit by a hammer when the piton is pounded into a crack. Below that is a hole called the eye. Leaf pitons are used in horizontal cracks. They do not hold nearly as well in vertical cracks, but in a horizontal one, a well-placed piton will hold about 4,000 pounds.

For larger cracks, from about ½ inch to 2½ inches wide, a V piton is normally used. Since it is the most commonly used of all pitons, it is also called the universal piton. As the name implies, the blade is in the shape of a V. As you pound it into a crack, the V begins to

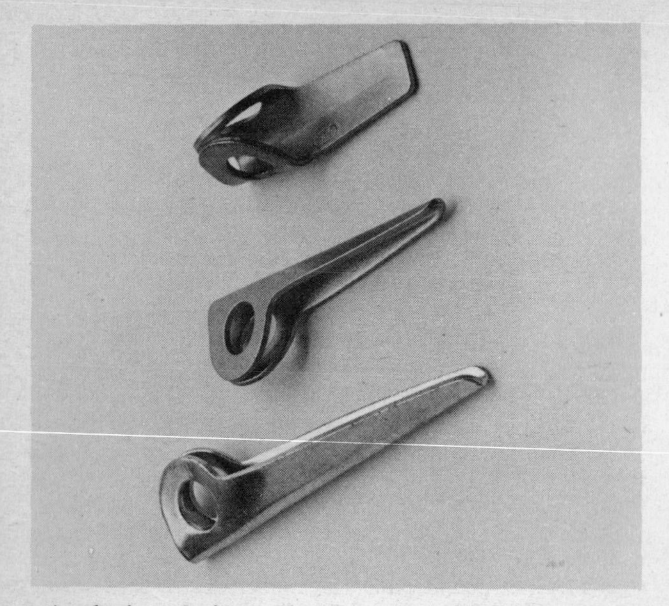

A selection of pitons. Shown are two angle pitons and a leaf piton. (*Courtesy Recreational Equipment, Inc.*)

flatten and grip the crack. The U-shaped piton is almost identical to the V piton, except that it is for slightly larger cracks.

For large cracks "bongs" are used. They do not look like other pitons. They are pieces of metal folded over and secured with a rivet. Each one has several eyes in it. Bongs were developed mainly for climbing in the Yosemite Valley. They fit cracks up to about four inches in width.

In general there are two types of cracks, horizontal and vertical. All things considered, pitons hold better in horizontal cracks than in vertical ones. In a horizontal crack the pull on a piton is against the rock, but this is not so in a vertical crack, where the piton may swivel. Occasionally you do not have any other choice but to use a vertical crack; so you should understand its limitations.

Pitons are frequently tougher than the rock. In placing a piton, you must consider the strength of the rock. There is no absolute way of knowing, of course, but you should avoid crumbly rock and rock that splinters if possible.

Another thing which effects the strength of a piton is the angle at which it is placed.

The nature of the crack can affect the way the piton holds. Some cracks have parallel walls. They hold a piton. Some cracks have walls which widen out the deeper they go into a cliff. Watch out for them. They hold a piton very poorly. The piton is supported by rock in the front, but in the back nothing is really holding it.

Some people mistakenly think they can tell how well a piton is holding by the sound it makes as it is hammered into a crack. Quite often the metal rings as it is hit. It is sometimes thought that the higher the pitch of the notes, the better it is holding. There is some truth to that, but it is not an acid test. It is true that a poorly placed piton may not sound right. The sound may be cloddy or dull. A well-placed one should give off a "ping" sound, and a poorly placed one may go "chunk." At any rate, always listen, in spite of the limitations of the test.

Once a piton is placed, check it. There is no way of

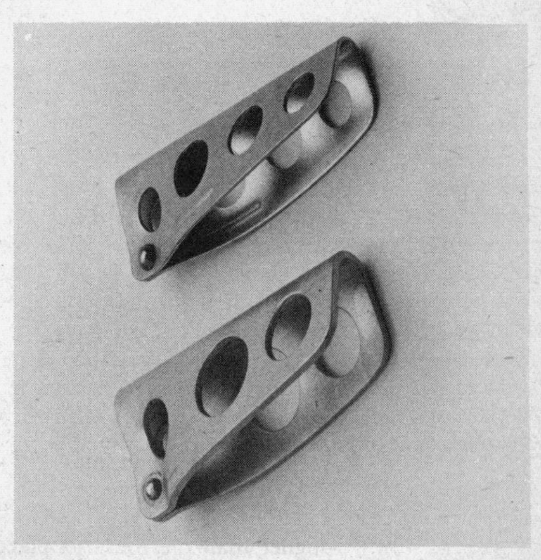

Bongs. (*Courtesy Recreational Equipment, Inc.*)

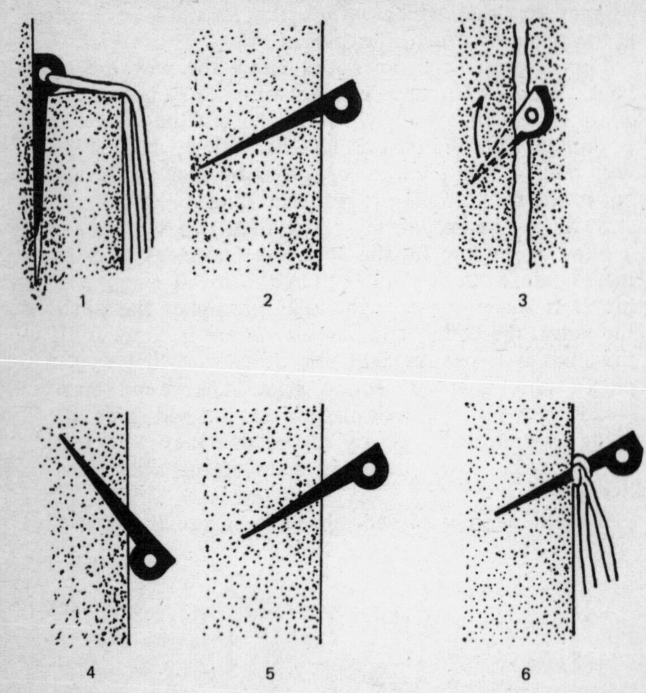

Illustration 1 shows a well-placed piton. A rope loop is placed in it, and a carabiner would be attached to the loop. Illustration 2 shows a well-placed piton. Illustration 3 shows a piton placed in a vertical crack; it could possibly swing when weight is placed on it. Illustration 4 shows a poorly placed piton; a downward pull could possibly pull it out. Illustration 5 shows a poorly placed piton; though it is slanted correctly, it is not deeply enough embedded in the crack. In Illustration 6 a rope loop is placed over the piton that is not deep enough in the crack. Weight against the rope would be better than through the eye, because the rope loop will put less leverage against the piton.

really knowing how well it is placed, but tap it lightly with the hammer on the edge. It should not budge. Hit it lightly up and then down and see what happens. It should feel firm. Be sure to look at the rock it is in. Sometimes a piton can crack a rock. Try to decide how strong the rock is, and look around the piton for any damage it may have caused.

All well-placed pitons are pounded in down to the eye. Occasionally, though, a crack is too shallow, and it is impossible to pound the piton in all the way. If so, do not trust the piton for a belay or as a major anchor point. A rope sling should be tied to the exposed piton blade and the carabiner attached to it. This will not put as much leverage against the piton.

Pitons are often reused. The last man up the cliff takes out the pitons which were used for the climb. Pitons are taken out by hitting them so that they begin to wobble back and forth in the crack. Every now and then a piton will be so secure that you cannot dislodge it without wasting too much time, so it has to be left.

Ice pitons do not look at all like rock pitons. Most look like long rods which have screw threads on them. Some are a foot long. They are placed in solid ice simply by screwing them into it.

Cold ice holds ice pitons better than ice around 32° F. Pitons in ice near the freezing point can hold only about 500–2,400 pounds, whereas in ice between 8° and 10° F they can hold from about 1,300 to over 5,000 pounds.

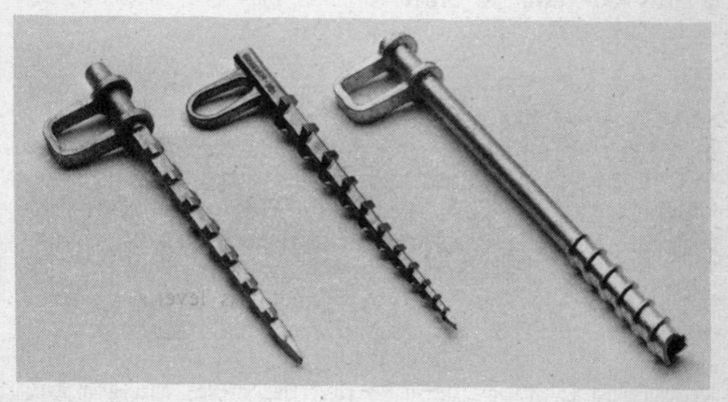

A selection of ice pitons. (*Courtesy Recreational Equipment, Inc.*)

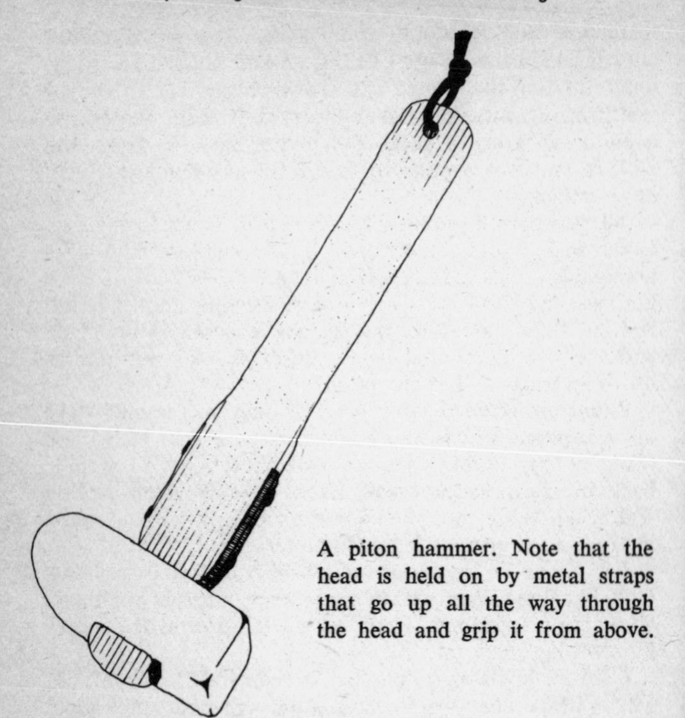

A piton hammer. Note that the head is held on by metal straps that go up all the way through the head and grip it from above.

The ice pitons should be placed with the points going slightly downhill. In other respects they are used as you would use a rock piton.

A household hammer is not used with pitons. A good piton hammer has several features. First of all, the hammer head is much heavier than a carpenter's hammer. The face of the hammer is wide and usually square. The wider face is obviously helpful in hitting the piton. At the other end of the hammer head there is usually a pick. It can be used for cleaning away dirt, lichens, and other things near and over a crack. The head of the hammer usually weighs about one pound and is held on by a strap of metal which goes along the handle. At the end of the strap is an L-shaped bend so that the metal can grip the head and hold it on. The metal strap along the handle helps to protect the handle. At the other end of the handle there is a hole, through which you run a strong nylon cord. The cord is secured to the climber so that the hammer, if it falls, can easily be retrieved.

Pitons are not the only items invented for placing in rock cracks for the purpose of holding carabiners and affording a secure holding point for a rope. Though beginners should use pitons first, they may want to know about other types of equipment.

One item is the "wedge." This is a piece of metal, usually aluminum, which can be fitted into a crack which narrows at the bottom. The piece of metal, as the name implies, is in the shape of a wedge. When placed in the crack it jams in there. At the base of the wedge is a bar or eye for attaching a carabiner. Such wedges have their limitations. They are only secure when there is a downward pressure on them. But a wedge is very strong, with holding power up to 6,500 pounds.

Hex nuts, or, as they are called in England, "chocks," are short sections of hexagonal pipe. They have holes drilled in them for placing steel wire or nylon webbing. Hex nuts are fitted into wide cracks. They jam in them very much like wedges. They are also strong. They are stronger than the wires, which hold up to about 2,600 pounds.

Stops or stoppers are made very much the same. They

A selection of "hexes" or hexentrics. They fit into cracks in the rocks. Perlon cords are placed through the holes and carabiners attached. (*Courtesy Recreational Equipment, Inc.*)

are wedge-shaped plugs with cables already attached. They are somewhat smaller than wedges or hex nuts and are used for smaller cracks.

Because pitons clutter up cracks and damage rocks, many climbers today are using hex nuts, stoppers, wedges, and so on. After using them, a climber can easily take them out of a rock crack. No damage will occur and the rock will look like new after the climbers have left. Some very difficult climbs have been done with such equipment.

There are a few other items which are now being developed for climbers. They need not be included. Most are in the experimental stage. And it is far better for beginners to learn how to use basic, standard equipment flawlessly before "graduating" to more difficult equipment.

Rock climbers must wear helmets to protect their heads from falling stones or from accidentally dropped hardware such as pitons, carabiners, and so on. Most rock climbing helmets look something like those worn by motorcyclists but are usually lighter weight. Some are more like hard hats. Get one with a chin strap so that it will not accidentally fall off. Be sure to get one large enough so that you can wear a warm cap under it.

Carabiners pronounced "care-a-beaners" are a type of snap link. Most are oval in shape, though many are D-shaped. Most are about two by four inches. At a distance they look like solid rings, but all carabiners have a

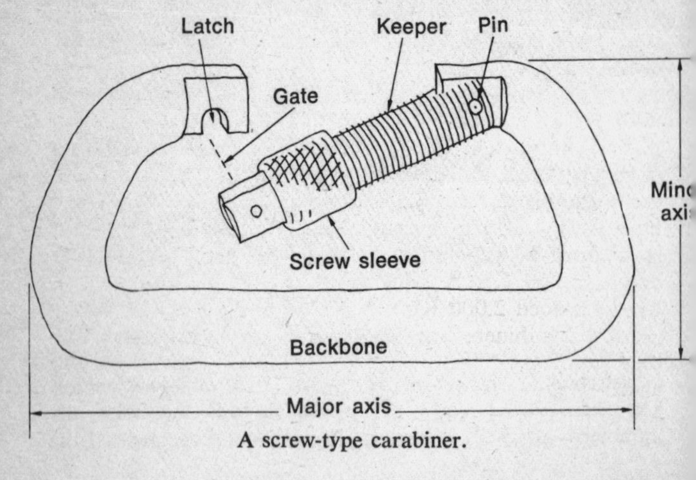

A screw-type carabiner.

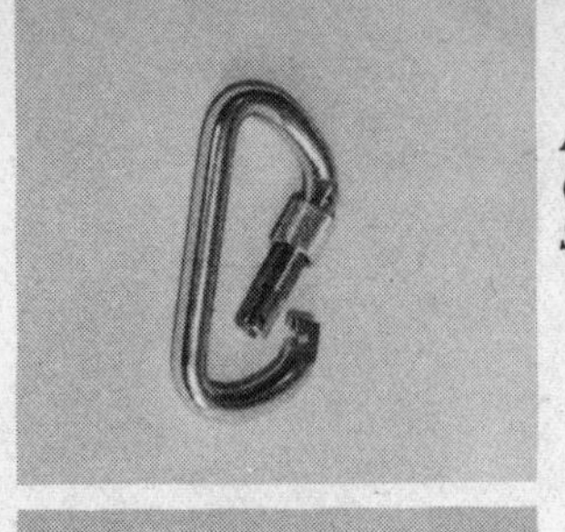

A screw-type carabiner, open. (*Photograph by Alexander Smith*)

A screw-type carabiner, closed and with the screw turned so that it will stay closed. (*Photograph by Alexander Smith*)

keeper which opens and closes. The keeper has a hinge on one end. The opening is called the gate. The hinge has a pin. The gate hooks into a latch. Some carabiners have a screw sleeve which can be turned in such a way that the keeper will stay closed.

All climbers need at least one carabiner which has a screw sleeve on it. This particular carabiner secures the climber to the climbing rope. It must be screwed tight so that it will not open accidentally. The other carabiners do not have a screw sleeve.

You cannot tell by the weight of a carabiner whether or not it is really strong. The shape of the carabiner and the metal used determine its strength. Many carabiners have their breaking strength stamped on them. Usually it is stamped in kilograms. A stamp will thus say, for example, 2,000 Kg. A kilogram is 2.2 pounds, so a carabiner stamped 2,000 Kg will hold 4,400 pounds.

Most carabiners are made of some sort of steel, so they may rust. They can also be affected by alkalis and acids. Many carabiners are coated with chrome, which helps to protect them. However, if they are used on sea cliffs where there is salt spray, they should be washed off

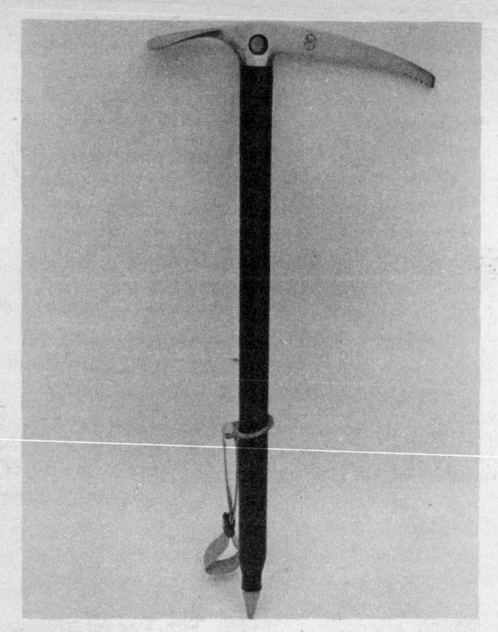

An ice axe. On the top is the head. To the left is the adze and to the right the pick. The hole is for attaching a carabiner. At the bottom is the spike. The shaft has a ring around it to which a strap is attached. A climber would keep the strap around his wrist. (*Courtesy Recreational Equipment, Inc.*)

with clean, fresh water. At all times check carabiners for rust.

When choosing a carabiner, be sure that the gate is large enough for all types of ropes that you might use. A good rule is to get one with at least an opening of ⅝ inch. For use on a glacier, the gate should be larger than an inch. One would think that a keeper which required a lot of pressure to open would be the safest. Actually, the keeper should be rather easy to open. That will save your strength and allow you to put ropes into the carabiner and hook it onto pitons quickly and easily.

If you ever climb on snow or ice, you will need an ice axe. Choose one of a height that will not tire you when you use it as a walking stick. To get the correct height, stand up straight and put your arm down, with your elbow slightly bent. Measure from the palm of your hand to the floor. Most ice axes are sold in lengths varying by two-inch increments from about twenty-four to forty inches. When you use the axe as a walking stick, the pick end should point forward, for if you fall, you don't want that pointed toward you.

An ice axe is made up of several parts. There is a shaft, which is oval in cross section. It can be made of very hard wood or of metal. The stronger the shaft the better. At the bottom of the shaft is a ferrule, which is a band of metal around the base. Inside it, pointing downward, is the spike. The spike is useful for "gripping" icy and snowy slopes and for probing deeply into snow for crevasses. It is frequently used to check snow conditions—for example, to see how deep a hard crust may be. It is also used for pushing clogged snow out of crampon points.

On top of the shaft is the head. At one end is an adze. The adze is used for cutting steps in hard snow or ice. At the other end of the head is the pick, which is useful in cutting into hard ice and for stopping a fall. Both the pick and the adze should be rather long. The head itself is of one solid piece of steel for strength. Most, but not all, heads have an eye in the center for placing a carabiner.

In buying an ice axe, first check the shaft. The only acceptable wood is hickory, and even it will last only four years or so. Then it will begin to lose strength. Stronger ice axes have metal shafts, which have a coating of plastic over them to keep down heat loss. Holding the metal head of an ice axe on a cold windy day can be very cold, as the metal drains heat away from the hand holding it.

If the ice axe has an eye in its head, you will have a place for a strap. The strap goes around your wrist so that you cannot lose the ice axe. If there is no hole in the head, then the shaft should have a screw stopper on it, an oval ring, and strap. Also, get protectors for the spike and head.

An ice axe with a hickory shaft should be replaced every four years. The spike, the pick, the serrated edges under it, and the adze should always be kept sharp. If they become dull, they should be filed until they are sharp. Quite frequently other parts of the ice axe, such as the top parts of the head may get nicked and burrs will form. The burrs can get sharp and cut gloves, so they must, of course, be filed down.

If you are going to be on steep slopes with hard snow or on ice, you will need crampons. Crampons are steel frames which fit on the bottom of climbing boots. At their base are downward-pointing sharp spikes or points which dig in and allow you to walk on the ice.

There are two types of crampons. One type, the ten-point vertical, has all the spikes pointing downward. The other, called the twelve-point horizontal or the lobster claw, has the same ten spikes pointing downward but also has two extra spikes which point directly forward from the toe.

In buying crampons, be sure that they fit the boot exactly. If they are too tight, you will always have trouble getting them on, especially in snowy conditions when you must do it with gloves. On the other hand, they cannot be too loose. If they are, you will lose confidence. The wobble can make you feel as though you will fall, and indeed can throw you off balance. In addition to all that, loose ones are excessively tiring. To be sure that the fit is correct put the crampons over the boot. The crampons should hug the boot and not slip off when the boot is raised from the floor. Usually you cannot get a perfect fit and the crampon supports must be bent. A good outfit which sells them by mail order will ask you to send them your boots and they will fit them and return the boots

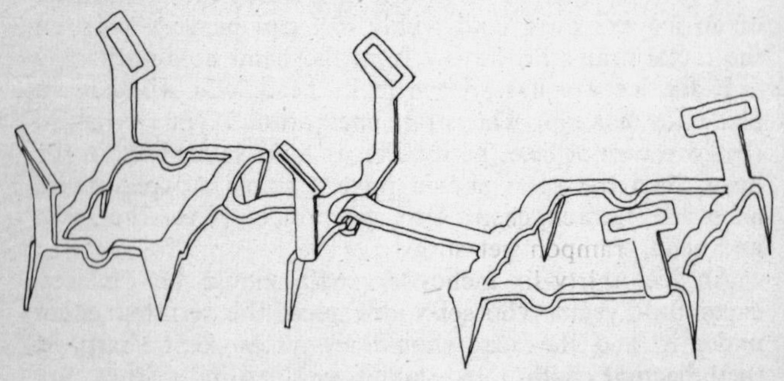

A crampon. The straps go through the eyes.

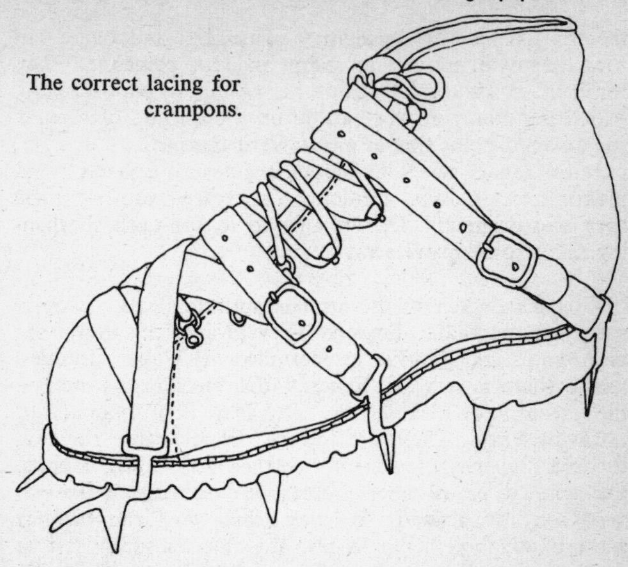

The correct lacing for crampons.

with the crampons. If a perfect fit is not obtained, do not try to climb with them.

A beginner will be far better off getting the regular ten-point vertical crampons rather than the lobster claw. The lobster claw can be dangerous. For example, if you fall and the lobster claws grab the ice too quickly, you can somersault. Furthermore, lobster claws are used only on extremely steep ice cliffs, which are beyond a beginner's capacity. So buy a ten-point vertical pair, with front points near the toe.

With crampons you will need straps. There are several ways of putting on the straps. You can put crampons on using one long strap or two shorter straps. The advantage in using the two shorter straps is that you can put them on and take them off faster, which at times is an important consideration. There are six rings on the crampons for the straps. Most straps are made of nylon coated with neoprene. Less expensive ones are made of nylon webbing. For each crampon get straps between 9⁄16 and 5⁄8 inch in width, one thirty-six inches long and the other forty-four inches long. Once you get your straps, practice with them so you can operate the crampons quickly and effectively on the actual climb.

To carry crampons, a climber needs rubber point protectors. The points are sharp and need to be covered so that they will not rip up packs or stab someone. Also, the rubber protectors keep the crampon points sharp. When the crampons are carried on the outside of a pack, the covered point should aim toward the pack.

If the points get dull, sharpen them with a file. Do not make them thin or needlelike, but close to the shape they had originally. Do not overdo it, for each sharpening takes some metal away.

Goggles are one of the most important pieces of equipment for mountain climbers. They protect the eyes from high winds and blowing ice particles. At higher altitudes, where there is less air, more of the sun's rays penetrate the atmosphere. There are also increased amounts of ultraviolet rays. These are the rays which cause the skin to burn and they are harmful to the eyes. Oddly enough, the worst days are when the sky is overcast and there is snow on the ground. At such times you can become snow blind, though that is also possible on sunny, bright days. Just as the name implies, snow blindness actually causes temporary blindness. A person suffering from it

Two climbers have on goggles to protect their eyes from the sun's glare on the snow. (*Courtsy Swiss National Tourist Office*)

will be totally incapacitated. Furthermore, a person who has suffered from it once will be more likely to get it again. Thus the extreme importance placed on goggles. At high altitudes one must wear goggles all the time, from sunup to sunset.

Goggles are specially designed to prevent snow blindness. Do not try to use dark glasses; they will not do the job. All goggles have lenses for protection against high-altitude rays. They have covers on the side so that no light comes in from the sides. Thus, no matter where you look, the eyes are protected. The sides are usually vented so that air can get into the inside of the goggles. If the air inside and outside of the lenses is the same temperature, the goggles will not mist over.

There are several types of goggles. In the best, 98 per cent of all ultraviolet and infrared rays are stopped by the lenses. Some goggles have two lenses, one for each eye. Others have one very large lens for both eyes. Those of the single-lens type are often large enough that they can be put on over eyeglasses. Most goggles have interchangeable lenses, so that broken lenses can be replaced quickly and so that you can put in different sorts of lenses. Some lenses are made of plastic. They have the advantage that they are cheaper and usually do not break too easily—though really cold plastic can become brittle. Glass lenses are more expensive, but they can be made so that there is no distortion, some can be prescription ground.

Most climbers take an extra set of goggles. There are some cheap ski goggles which can be bought for about three dollars or less. Some can be folded up and kept in the pocket of your shirt.

If you are ever so unfortunate that the lenses break in your last pair of goggles, you can put tape across the opening with a small horizontal slit left to see through. In an emergency, you can make a cloth blindfold and cut two slits in it.

With all goggles, misting is a problem. If the side vents of a pair of goggles are too open, wind can get through. If they are too airtight, misting becomes more of a problem. There are antimisting compounds made. They form a thin film over the glass or plastic on the inside. It is said that soap rubbed on glass and then rubbed down until it is invisible will work fairly well.

10

Miscellaneous Items

COMPASS. A compass is a must item. In choosing one, look for strength first. A compass needle which ceases to function or which falls off the pin is useless. Next, see that it is obvious which end of the needle points north. If it is doubtful, mark on the back of the compass which end does. My advice is to get a compass which is easy to use. Too many people get ultrafancy things. For years I worked as a surveyor, and the compass I used, which cost more than five hundred dollars, was far simpler than many I have seen advertised by camping supply houses.

Get a compass which you feel comfortable with and which is handy. A compass is often set on top of a map to obtain a bearing, thus those with a straight edge along the side are better than round compasses. A compass with a see-through plastic base is good, as one can see the map under it and get a better bearing. Most compasses have a pointer which can be turned for a bearing. I think any compass for a mountain climber should have a cord so

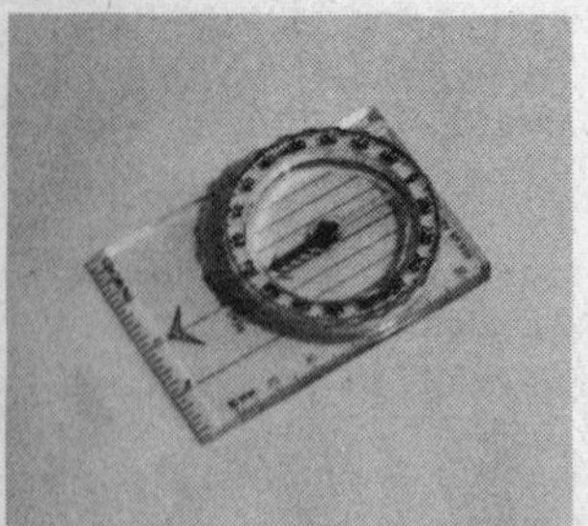

A compass suitable for mountain climbing and wilderness use. Note that the dial is on a transparent base. The whole dial can be turned, which is handy for route-finding work. (*Photograph by Alexander Smith*)

that you can attach it to your clothing and not accidentally lose it.

Most compasses have a sighting arrow. You point the arrow toward the place you wish to walk and follow it. For most work this is good enough. Other, more expensive compasses have sights or a mirror which serves as a sight. With such compasses one can obtain a greater degree of accuracy.

KNIVES. Do not take a "hunting knife" which goes into a sheath. For most things they are useless. They were actually made for hunting—not camping.

A mountain climber needs a good knife for camping, cooking, eating, and for cutting ropes. The best all-around knife is a jackknife. What you look for is sturdiness. Never get one with a weak and wobbly blade. The more blades, the worse the knife is. Forget about attachments: bottle openers, awls, and all of that. They only weaken the knife. Get a good knife with only two blades at the most. No one seems to make a good one with a loop such as the old boy-scout knives had so that you can attach a cord to the knife. When buying the knife, take the blade from behind and try to wiggle it. Test its strength.

The blade should be made of good steel which will hold a sharp cutting edge. It is very difficult to tell whether you are looking at a knife with good steel or not. The only way is to sharpen it and use it. Carbon steel will sharpen the best, but in my experience, various knives—all of carbon steel—were different. Some had much better steel than others.

You will need, more than most campers, to keep the knife sharp. When using it on ropes, you do not want to find the knife is too dull.

Knife sharpening, I think, is sort of an art. You cannot quite show anyone how it is done. The only way to learn is through a lot of practice. Get a good whetstone; those from Arkansas are supposedly the best. The stone is wetted or oiled before use. The liquid takes away any buildup of heat from the blade. Some stones are more closely textured than others. The closer the texture, the sharper you can make the blade. On the other hand, a closely textured stone will not grind away enough steel for the beginning phases of the work at hand. The answer is to get a stone with two faces, one with a closely textured face and the other side coarser.

To sharpen the knife, wet the stone or spit on it and hold the knife blade against it. Hold the edge against the stone so that the face of the blade makes about a twenty- to thirty-degree angle with the stone. The less the angle is, the sharper but more brittle the edge. Once you decide on the angle, the trick is to keep it in all subsequent motions. On the wet stone, move the knife in circular motions. If your touch is too light, the stone won't file the knife down. If it is too hard, the knife will heat up too much and the edge will be rough and uneven. You can feel the stone eat away at the knife.

Grind the knife with nice even motions, trying all the time for an evenness of pressure and of angle. After a while turn the knife over and grind the other side on the same face of the stone. Repeat the whole process about three times. Always see that the stone is wet. Carefully clean the knife. Push a damp cloth along the blade. Watch your fingers. Look carefully into the cloth. If the steel has been ground down, there will be tiny particles of dark gray steel on the cloth. This indicates you are doing everything correctly, though it is not an acid test. Be sure the knife is clean before going to the next face of the stone where the texture is smoother.

Do the whole thing over. This time there will be a burr on the knife's edge. You can feel it by placing your finger on the face of the knife and slowly moving it lightly toward the blade. Do it on both sides. You'll no doubt feel it. Very carefully, with a couple of light strokes, grind it off with the smooth side of the stone. Once more, clean the blade with a damp cloth. If you have an old belt, you can strop the blade, but don't do it if you think you might cut the belt.

Is it sharp? To find out, take a piece of paper. Hold it up and gently draw the knife over its edge. If the knife is sharp, it will easily cut the paper. Do not repeat. Paper actually dulls knives. Another way of telling is that sharp knives grip meat or wood as they cut it.

Do not use a sharp knife unless you have to. It is all too easy to cut yourself. For butter and cheese it is sometimes best to carry just a plain dull table knife.

Since a knife is an emergency item, it must be kept on you. If it has a metal loop to which a string or thong can be tied, all the better. Otherwise it should be kept deep in a pants pocket, or a small sheath should be made for it and placed on the belt.

MATCHES. Most camping stores carry metal matchboxes which are waterproof. They are probably worth it. Matches can also be kept in a small plastic bottle, however, or in a small plastic bag secured with a rubber band.

Always take a few hundred more matches than you think you'll need. Keep some in pants pockets, others in shirt pockets, and others in your pack. The best are wooden kitchen matches. They can be waterproofed with shellac or paraffin. Paper book matches are often used, but for me they are a second choice. They cannot be waterproofed. Kitchen matches strike anywhere, and are easier to light. The flame of the kitchen match lasts longer. Also, paper matches can bend down and burn you more easily. Yet, they can be carried in a plastic bottle, which will keep them waterproof.

LIGHTS. At the very best, camp lighting is poor. Mountain climbers cannot take along a gasoline lamp, for the mantle is too fragile and the whole lamp is too heavy. The same goes for a propane lamp. Candles are too weak, though so foolproof that many people carry them.

There are only two satisfactory solutions. The easiest thing to do is to carry a small flashlight powered by alkaline cells, which last much longer than regular cells. Such a flashlight is handy, quite reliable (though not perfect), and lightweight, but it throws only a narrow beam. Only those things right in front of the beam can be seen. Take along extra flashlight bulbs and batteries if there is a possibility they will be needed.

The other solution is to obtain a carbide headlamp. For many years these were used by miners. The light in them comes from an intense white open flame. Behind the flame is a parabolic mirror, which concentrates the light into a beam. The fuel for the flame comes from the reaction of water and carbide. One pound of carbide will burn in the lamp for 25.6 hours. The headlamps are a bit tricky and need some attention, though I've found them reliable. You have to put in new carbide and take out old carbide every now and then, which is okay, but the carbide has a strange, slightly sickening smell. However, you get more light from them, and on a weight basis—especially for a long trip—you do better with them. My choice has usually been to carry one.

SURVIVAL KITS. Ready-made kits are available. Some have fishing lines, hooks, etc. I do not know what to think of them. It has been my experience that fish are difficult to catch even under the best of circumstances with good equipment. Other kits have "space blankets." These are made of materials which are extremely lightweight but have aluminum on them. The metal reflects heat. Thus, when you are in the blanket, it reflects your body heat back on you and you stay warm. It could be handy, but most climbers already are dressed for extremely cold weather. Most kits have medicines, but they would already be carried in a first aid kit. Others have food, but again you would have your own. It seems that the items in a survival kit are things you would already have with you anyway. But if such a kit gives you a sense of security, take one along.

MIRROR. Many survival kits contain a mirror which is used for signaling airplanes. You can easily buy such mirrors separately as well. Since a mirror is handy, maybe you should take along one which serves two purposes—as a signal mirror and to use for checking yourself for ticks and other sores.

WHISTLE. I have always carried a whistle. If you are lost, you can whistle and searchers, hopefully, will hear you. At times, a whistle is handy for sending prearranged signals from one group to another.

CORD. Cord is always handy. Nylon cord about ⅛ inch in diameter is good to have for wrapping things, hanging belongings in trees, lashings, and so on. Take at least one hundred feet of it.

PLASTIC WATER JUG. This is an "iffy" item. I can see using a folding plastic jug which can hold a gallon or more of water in some places, but it would probably not be needed in most areas.

TOILET PAPER. Toilet paper is a needed item. Take along a roll. Take along a small plastic bag to carry it in.

SOAP. It is always difficult to keep clean on any camping trip and especially so in cold climates. Take along a bar of biodegradable soap.

WALLET. Take along a wallet with your identification, credit cards, or whatever else is needed.

PASSPORT. In foreign countries you will need to have a passport. In some countries the local police can be very demanding. The best thing may be to put it in a waterproof plastic bag and carry it flat around your neck at all times.

COINS. Always have coins for pay telephones. This is especially important if you ever need quick aid for a sick or injured person.

NOTEBOOK AND PENCILS. Take a small, lightweight notebook and a pencil or two. Do not take pens. At high altitudes they can leak due to pressure changes. In the notebook mark off, as carefully as possible, an inch scale and make some sort of rule. Also mark the time of sunrise and sunset for the days you will be camping, and the same for the planets and the moon. This can be handy for setting a stopped watch.

11

Party Organization and Leadership for Safety

The most basic rule in mountain climbing is that one never goes alone. Of course, many people have broken this rule, gone out for a long hike in the hills, and returned. On the other hand, some people have never returned. The trouble with solitary mountain climbing is that it takes so very little to keep a person from returning. A sprained ankle is enough at times. Thus, in a true sense, mountain climbing is a group sport. In fact, it is, in my opinion, the ultimate group sport. Mountain climbers safeguard each other's lives all day long. Who can say that for another sport?

In organizing a party of mountain climbers, take into consideration the number of people going, the type of mountain to be climbed, and the difficulty of the climb. Rock climbers, roped together, go in groups of two or three. Larger groups, roped together, can cross glaciers. A very large group of, say, twenty people who are climbing in a high mountainous region where there are no technical difficulties may rope together during severe weather conditions, such as during a blizzard.

During the summertime a large group of people can get together and climb an easy mountain on which they will find no technical problems. Any group larger than about a dozen people seems to me too large. It has been my experience that smaller groups have more fun.

Groups should be made up of people more or less equal in strength and experience. Almost all mountain clubs have easy climbs for beginners and more difficult climbs for more experienced people. All climbs are graded in some manner. For example, some are short hikes, some very long treks; others are rock climbing trips on difficult cliffs; others may be trips in severe winter weather. Everyone should try to fit into the right group. Before a group goes on a climb, the difficulties of the climb should be thoroughly discussed. No one should ever hesitate to ask questions about it.

Before any group goes on a climb, someone should notify a friend and tell him where the group is going, what the route will be, what time they intend to leave, and what time they expect to get back. The hour of a planned return is important. If a group is overdue, then some people should be sent to find them. That group, in turn, should notify people that they are out rescuing others. No group should ever be in the mountains without someone back in civilization knowing of their whereabouts.

All groups should choose a leader. In a very real way a leaderless group is not a group at all. In choosing one, be sure the person is qualified. The leader should know the region, or should be a better climber than the others, or he should be a more responsible type than the others. Responsibility is the most important factor. In many mountain clubs the leaders are somewhat certified. The club will have rules for choosing them, mostly on the basis of experience.

Once the leader is chosen, the climb should be discussed. If anyone has questions, they ask. If the leader has any questions about someone's ability to go on a specific climb, the person should be questioned to find out if he is qualified. If not, the leader should politely say that he cannot go on that given trip. A person can be disqualified because he will not follow rules, is inexperienced, is not strong enough for the given climb, or is too much of a troublemaker. Whatever the reason, one person cannot be allowed to ruin a good climb for everyone else.

It is usually the leader's responsibility to notify someone outside of the group of the group's planned trip. The leader should appoint a helper who will be second in charge of the group. A leader will describe as best he can the nature of the trip. He will also discuss the weather and what conditions will be expected. He and the group will discuss, in detail, all the equipment needed for the trip. This means everything from sleeping bags to peanuts, from face masks to pitons. At the end of the discussion, every single member will know exactly what he is supposed to bring on the trip.

Transportation must be considered. In almost all instances group members must drive in automobiles to the trail. The whole thing must be discussed. Once assigned to a certain automobile, one should not change over to another. If someone does not show up for the trip, that is the quickest way of finding out. Also, in case someone is left in the hills, the automobile arrangements will indicate that—in spite of the fact that in any good group it should not happen.

The final meeting place where the trail begins must be discussed in great detail, especially if most people have never been there before. The leader and drivers must study a map. Even that does not always work. Trails are sometimes so poorly marked and country roads can be so confusing that it is often wise to leave markers. The car with the leader goes ahead by an hour or so and leaves some temporary marker at confusing crossroads. It can be a bandana tied to a tree, a note in a bottle placed at the base of a fence post, or whatever. The other drivers can pick up the markers.

A time is set for everyone to meet. This is usually early in the morning. Before anyone gets into automobiles, everyone is accounted for. Some people may be sick that day or not appear for other reasons. People who are not going to show up should make every possible effort to inform the group beforehand.

If people meet at a bus station or railroad station, all should be counted just before getting in the buses. The leader will also check to see that everyone has the right equipment. Those who do not should not go on the trip. Once all those details are taken care of, everyone leaves.

At the next bus station or at the trail where all the automobiles meet, everyone is once more counted.

When all the group have put on their packs and adjusted their boots, the leader should start the trip. At the very last minute he should check the weather. If a storm is approaching, he must call the whole thing off. That is one of the great non-joys of mountain climbing—after you have gotten everything together, dragged yourself out of bed at five o'clock in the morning, and driven for three hours.

It is, of course, up to the leader actually to lead. He

chooses the route, sets the pace, and in general, decides everything. Of course, a good leader is not a tyrant. Indeed it is his responsibility to keep a sense of humor and see to it that the trip is pleasant. The trip should benefit the greatest number.

On the trail, the second-in-charge has an important job. He is as qualified as, or may even be more qualified than the leader. He stays behind the group and follows it as last person, always seeing to it that the group stays together. Of all things, that is the most important. No one should ever leave the group. He also sees that the pace set by the leader is correct. If it is too fast, the leader is notified of that. If someone needs to stop, the second-in-charge should ask the leader to stop the group. Often it is easiest, if the group is large, for the second to arrange a whistle code with the leader.

In one respect it is the leader's job to look ahead, always checking routes and weather, always looking for danger or ways of making the trip easier for people. The second-in-charge focuses attention on the group, constantly watching the people to see that they are all right.

If a group is well-led and well-followed, the people in it will feel more secure and have a happier trip. It is the responsibility of the two leaders to make the people feel good.

Each mountain climbing trip, in my opinion, should be educational. Anyone who has any knowledge of the geology, animal life, or plants of the region should speak up and discuss it. The leaders should encourage all such discussions. The more a mountain climber learns about the environment, how mountains are formed, what animals live there, what plants are edible, which produce the best firewood, and so forth, the better mountain climber he will be. Such topics really do make a mountain climb much more enjoyable.

At any time a leader should be able to call the climb off. On the other hand, he should have a good idea of the strength of the group. On some days people simply seem stronger than on others, and the same goes for groups. I recall one day when a group of mountain climbers were out, we all felt so good that we climbed two peaks instead of one. For some unknown reason we were all in great shape and in good spirits, and in addition the weather was rather warm. A group should be able to change plans. Of course the leader must discuss all changes of plan. Some people may have to be back in town at a certain hour and have appointments they cannot miss. The leader has no right to extend a trip against anyone's wishes.

If anyone is injured, the leader, with the group's consent, must immediately decide what to do. Of course the person most knowledgeable in first aid will need to help the injured person. The leader should designate two or three strong and swift people from the group to leave the group and go back to a telephone and get help. The rest of the group should stay together. At such a time the leader may decide on a better way back. The easiest route out of the hills should be taken, of course, and this must be explained to those going for help.

During times of bad weather the leader should decide whether or not to take refuge or get the group tied together on a rope.

On any normal trip, free of any complications, the leader and second-in-charge should try in every way to teach beginners how to mountain climb. The very best way for a beginner to learn how to climb—indeed, the only way—is to go along with good leaders. Ask them to explain things. Always question them about techniques.

All during a trip people are accounted for on a regular basis. At the very end of the trip people are once more accounted for. The leader's responsibilities are over, more or less, at the end of the trail when people get into their automobiles to go home. Yet leaders should carefully consider the drivers. Mountain climbing is exhausting work. At times people who have been climbing all day and then are driving home have gone to sleep at the wheel. If the leaders feel drivers are too tired, they should suggest that less tired people drive or that the group camp out that night or go to a nearby hotel and get a good night's sleep before heading back.

Everyone on a trip should, of course, help the leader as much as possible. They should be responsible for good cheer. Another way of helping the leader and the group is not to complain. I think I have been very fortunate; very few of the climbers I have been with ever complained, even under extremely trying conditions.

All people in a group should try in every way to be extremely careful of the environment. I would say that of all groups, mountain climbers have been the most careful to see that no litter is left, that plants are not needlessly touched, animals annoyed, or trails and routes up cliffs changed from their natural state.

One of the greatest things about mountain climbing groups is that the people in them often become lasting friends. Perhaps it is because everyone shares in a common experience, or maybe it is because, at times, you put your life in the hands of another person.

12

The First Big Climb

Most people who have become good mountain climbers have followed a pattern. First, they were vaguely interested in mountain climbing; then they went on some hikes, and later went with a mountain club group. Then they decided to try a big climb with two or three companions.

When two or three people decide to go on a big climb, they already know something about hiking and mountain climbing. They also know what is expected of leadership and groups. Of course, if three people go together and they are all equally experienced, the idea of a leader is not as significant as with a large group. On the other hand, one person is usually more experienced and should in a democratic way serve as the leader. At a minimum the people should all discuss who will be responsible for what. Who is going to provide transportation? Who is going to notify people of the group's whereabouts? Who is going to cook? Who is going to put up the tent? It is always best to iron major things out first. With two, three, or four people it is rarely a problem.

Most beginners choose for their first mountain one which is high enough in altitude to be exciting but which does not present any technical difficulties. Any big mountain above around 3,000 feet will do. (Some mountain clubs refuse to acknowledge a climb unless the people who made it ascended at least 3,000 feet. Let us take an example. Pikes Peak is 14,110 feet above sea level. There is a road to the top of it. If a person drove an automobile up to 11,110 feet above sea level on that road and then climbed the peak, it would rate as a climb. If he drove up to a point 13,000 feet above sea level and hiked to the top it would not rate as a climb. Thus, a climb is an ascent of 3,000 or more feet, which most people consider to be a fair way of deciding what is a nontechnical climb and what is not. Of course, a technical climb is a different story altogether.) You can find many big mountains from 3,000 feet above sea level to some over 19,000 feet high, such as Kilimanjaro of Africa which soars 19,340 feet into the air. From all accounts, one can simply walk up it without any technical mountain climbing knowledge. Thus, a person in excellent physical shape can hike to the top—as physically difficult as the trip may be.

Many mountains which are only big mounds are extremely interesting to climb. Many have fascinating geological features. Others have interesting wildlife or extraordinary plants. All high mountains introduce you to the rarefied world of high altitudes. In places above timberline you can be in Arctic conditions. Moreover, because of the lack of air, some high mountains are far harder to climb in terms of energy than those requiring technical skills. Best of all, some mountains afford vistas which you can never forget, they are so dramatic and beautiful.

Let us consider, as an example, a rather high but easy mountain, and one which offers some challenges, Mount Massive, 14,421 feet above sea level. It is the second highest peak in Colorado and the third highest summit in the forty-eight states south of Canada. In terms of height it should please any beginner, as it is considerably higher than Fujiyama, which is 12,388 feet high. It is also higher than Pikes Peak, which is 14,110 feet high. It is only 269 feet lower than the Matterhorn.

Before planning the climb of a big mountain like Mount Massive, you must know what sort of weather conditions can be expected. Mount Massive, being in the northern hemisphere at a latitude of about 39° N, will have severe cold weather most of the year at such an altitude. During the winter, temperatures at the summit can drop more than fifty below zero and high winds will rake it. Though an easy climb in the summer, it can be almost impossible and extraordinarily dangerous in the winter. Mount Massive, like many peaks in America and Canada, is climbable by beginners only during the late summer months. June would usually be too early to climb it, as there would still be deep snow. Worse, the snow could

Longs Peak, 14,255 feet above sea level, Colorado. A high peak such as this makes an excellent first climb. Though the face seen in the picture is difficult and would challenge an expert climber, there is a much easier route to the top to the right of the peak. (*Photograph by the author*)

be slushy and hard to manage, and there could still be some danger from cornices falling. These are snowy projections usually found near ridges. They overhang a slope and can fall on a climber. Some cornices weigh thousands of tons and can shoot for miles down a slope. By July the mountain should be free of most snow, but not all of it. August and September would be even better months. In October, however, there may be heavy snowfalls. This pattern is characteristic of most high mountains in the U.S. Rockies and the Sierra Nevada.

Once you have determined the peak, you should get a good topographic map of the region. Such maps are put out by the U. S. Geological Survey. You can obtain one by sending a letter or postcard to Map Information Office, U. S. Geological Survey, General Services Building, 18th and F Streets NW, Washington, D.C. 20405. Before any trip, you should study the map and get a mental picture of the region, knowing where peaks, towns, rivers, and roads are located. Of course, the peak itself should be carefully studied and a route planned.

Next, you should get all your equipment together.

It is best to carry a small notebook and a couple of sharpened pencils. Along with other useful data (see chapter 10, "Miscellaneous Items"), make a list in your notebook of other peaks that should be visible from the summit you are going to climb.

If you live in a town which is already at a high elevation, such as Santa Fe, New Mexico, or Boulder, Colorado, you will not have to get acclimated to a higher elevation. On the other hand, if you drive to Colorado from a sea level town where you have stayed awhile, you had better take the climb in two steps. Drive to a place like Leadville, which is located at an elevation of over 10,000 feet above sea level, and spend a couple of days there. This will give you time to adjust to higher altitudes.

One of the most difficult things in mountain climbing is getting started on the correct trail. Trails rarely have any indication whether they will lead to the summit of a mountain. Asking local people is often a waste of time. People who live among mountains are rarely interested in climbing them. They really do not know, in general, how to get to the peaks. The best thing to do is to put all your trust on a government topographical map and your own good common sense. With some chagrin I will confess a secret: Twice I have gotten on the wrong trail and climbed the wrong mountain—though one mistake proved to be marvelous. One of the most interesting climbs was on Marble Mountain, which I mistook for Humboldt Peak.

Thus, the first step can be wrong and all trips start with that first step. If you happen to make an error, however, you can turn back, or you may decide that the mistaken trail leads to something interesting and continue. When my companions and I discovered we were not on Humboldt, we decided to continue toward Marble Mountain. As a climber, you will probably some day have to make the same choice. Actually, the only time you should turn back is if the trail leads you toward dangerous-looking country, or if you have told people where you are going and feel that they could be misled if they were to look for you and you had gone someplace else. Take all into consideration.

Once you have found what you think is the right trail, pause and double-check everything. Do not proceed unless you are as certain as you can possibly be. As experience will show you, most trails are blind. That is, by standing at the beginning you cannot see where the trail will lead. Very rarely can you see the summit you want from the beginning of the trail.

When you begin hiking on the chosen trail, etch the beginning in your memory so that when you return you will know when you are near the end of the hike. Look forward and backward on the trail so that you have seen it from both directions. As you continue, turn around every now and then and memorize the trail as you go. Many years ago, I got a good piece of advice: When in the woods on a trail, look for unusual items—a tree broken in a strange way, a cliff with unusually colored rocks, a peculiar twist in a stream. Unusual things are far easier to remember. If you later get mixed up about the trail and find the items once more, you will know you are on the right trail back.

As you hike along, try to think about the geology of the region—where the streams go and where the nearest divide is, for example. Also note all the changes in vegetation. As you hike up a high mountain like Mount Massive, you will pass through many types of forests. Sooner or later you will recognize different forests as indicating different elevations. After a while such forests can serve you as guideposts, showing you within a few hundred feet how high you are.

If you happen to get a good view of the mountain and you are closer to it than before, stop and study it. Get its shape in mind. Always try to do this while the mountain is some distance from you. Often at closer distances you cannot see the mountain as well, or much detail will be lost by ridges and slopes. Only at a distance can you see the mountain as an entity.

While studying it, try to determine as best you can the route you will take to the summit. On a difficult peak this is a necessary operation. In fact, climbers sometimes study big peaks months before climbing them, making a special trip just to look at the peak before any attempt is made. Whymper, for example, who first climbed the

Matterhorn, took many trips out just to study the peak and its structure and to seek possible routes up it. Of course, Mount Massive does not deserve such attention. However, some study of it will save time later on. Moreover, it is good practice. Each time you study a peak before climbing it, the better you will become at route finding, a principle skill of a good mountain climber.

Set a pace and try to stick to it. About two hours before it gets dark, look for a camping place. Do not wait too long, or you may go by really good ones and wind up in a third-rate place. And, of course, do not wait until it is dark, as it will be very difficult to set up a camp in the dark.

Most places today have well-defined camping areas which the government has indicated. When I climbed Mount Massive, taking the trail from the east toward it, there was no such area. So what did I look for in a good camping place?

First you need water, so the place will be near a good water supply. If you are doubtful about the purity of the water supply, make a small campfire and boil the water in a metal cup. Next, look for possible annoying insects. Check out anthills or bushes where mosquitoes and ticks can hide. See if there are wasps or bees around. They usually appear quickly at the smell of food. The best places are places where there is a slight breeze blowing, but do not choose a place that is too exposed. A light breeze will help keep away flying insects. A few trees are handy for hanging food out of reach of animals such as porcupines. If you want a fire, be sure that there is a supply of firewood nearby. Last, but certainly not least, obtain a place with a good view of the mountains. Many campers, for reasons unknown, will put up a tent inside a grove of trees away from a great view. They have come a long way to be in the mountains; why not enjoy them? I like a place with a good view and also where I can watch the stars, moon, and planets at night.

Once you have decided on a camping place, find a spot for the sleeping bags. Clean off the ground. Hang up the pack by a cord from a tree branch so that animals will not be able to get into it and eat the food. Some people carry along a light-weight nylon net bag, place their food in it, hang it, and keep their knapsacks near them at night. When you put your boots up for the night, place them on two sticks pushed in the ground. Point the soles toward the sky so that if it rains, your boots will not get water in them. If you have an ice axe, hang it from a tree. Animals like the salt from the sweat on the handle.

As you lie in your sleeping bag at night, you will hear all sorts of noises. You'll wonder if someone opened up the local zoo. Porcupines are common and so are skunks. You can push porcupines away with a stick. Do not kill them as it's cruel and happens to be illegal. Skunks are bold and I know of no way to get rid of them. On the other hand, they are at most camping places and I've never been sprayed.

Many people do not sleep well the first night out on a trip. Be sure you have gotten a good night's sleep the night before. If you have a bad night, just remember that most people have them at first. Try to wake up early, just before dawn. Without an alarm clock it can be rough. Do your best. Do all things smoothly and rapidly. Get breakfast down and the knapsacks packed and get ready to go on as soon as you can. Time saved in the morning is valuable.

Just before leaving, see to it that you have filled up your canteen. Take one last-minute check around the camping area to be sure you did not leave anything. Also, see to it that the place is cleaner than when you arrived.

Mountain climbing is mostly a matter of stamina, at least in climbing a peak like Mount Massive, which calls for quite a bit of it. Rank beginners almost always start off too fast. An even pace with few rest stops will do it. Remember to walk slowly enough to carry on a conversation. In fact, you should feel as though you are holding yourself back. Get set for a long, hard grind.

Many people starting off on a cool morning and heading for a snowy, cold-looking peak overdress. An hour or two later they are sweating and either have to stop and change or get chilled. It is better to hike on the cool side. Not only can sweating be annoying, but it can cause the body to lose valuable salts; it slows down; and it can cause a chill later on. When dressing cool, hike with loose clothing.

The question always arises, when should you stop and rest? You want to remember what was said in the first chapter, "How to Walk."

As you slowly ascend the trail, keep a constant lookout for weather changes. Look for any signs of bad weather approaching. This usually means a sudden shift in the wind from one direction to another, or a sudden change in the wind velocity. Another bad sign is clouds gathering on mountaintops, even if the sky is clear. The one thing you can ignore is the cooling of the air. As you climb higher the air will almost invariably get noticeably colder.

Retreat if bad weather is brewing, especially if you see signs of a thunderstorm, which approaches with the buildup of big "thunderheads," which are towering clouds topped with a cauliflower-looking summit. Another time to move away is if layers of clouds form over the tops of the mountains and then slowly move downward. Any rain in the mountains during summertime can bring lightning, which is the most dangerous of all conditions for a mountain climber. Occasionally summer blizzards will hit in mountainous regions. Colorado Springs' biggest blizzard hit on July 4 and the city is only 6,000 feet above sea level.

As you go up the trail, speak to everyone you meet coming down it. Always ask such people what the trail ahead is like. This is not only polite, but expected. What you will be trying to find out is whether or not part of the trail is blocked by snowdrifts, whether streams are so full of water as to be next to impossible to ford, whether many trees have fallen down, and so forth.

Of course, even in the middle of summer you can come up to big deep snowdrifts which do cover the trail. When you do, you should check them out. First of all, see if anyone has crossed them. See how soft the snow is. Will you sink to your ankles, knees, or waist? Deep summer snowdrifts on Longs Peak stopped me after I fell in them time and time again up to my waist. The trouble with really large drifts is that you cannot tell how far they extend up a trail. Three hundred feet? Half a mile? Two miles? When faced with a snowdrift which causes you to flounder, try it at least to see if luck is with you. Perhaps in two or three hundred feet its crust gets hard so you can walk on it without sinking. Perhaps five hundred feet ahead the snowdrift has melted completely away. In fighting snow, do not become so exhausted that you have difficulty turning around and battling your way back out.

Snow, even snow in a forest, can at times cause glare. It is usual to put on goggles above the timberline, or right at timberline, but if the sun is shining on the snow and causing any glare, it would be best to put them on sooner.

The trail to Mount Massive disappears at around timberline. From there on, you are on your own. That is why I chose it as a sample peak. The question arises, what do you do when the trail gives out? In the case of Mount Massive you can see the summit ahead. In choosing the route toward an easy summit, you try to find one that will constantly gain altitude. You do not want to go up and then at some point be forced to go downhill and then up again. At high altitudes where you fight for every inch upward, it is pyschologically very difficult to go down, lose part of the gain, and start again. Do not choose too steep a route. Choose the most comfortable, which boils down to a compromise between a short route and a very steep one.

Avoid crossing through snowdrifts, and stay away from steep cliffs. Do not walk directly under them, as falling rocks are frequent. Stay away from the edges. Look for cornices, and avoid being under them. If you need drinking water, go below snowdrifts for it. If you wish to walk on dry ground, go above them.

Study the mountain. There are apt to be a maze of cliffs to avoid. Plan your route before moving onward. On Mount Massive there are several choices, but pick one and stick to it if you can.

On slopes above timberline, trees no longer block the wind. On most days you find a marked cooling at the timberline. Some people, on first entering into areas above timberline, are somewhat shocked at seeing a place so cold and barren and windswept. They can also be surprised at how large the area is. Seen from its base, a mountain's higher areas are foreshortened due to the slope and perspective of the mountain. Also, you can be surprised to be at such a high elevation—12,500 feet, more or less, above sea level—and see the summit still so far away.

Most climbers stop a few feet above timberline and change into warmer clothes. As they move forward once more, they will begin to feel the effects of high altitude. The air is thinner and breathing becomes slightly more difficult. The pace will be slower. Put on goggles.

A mountain in the Colorado Rockies. It would be dangerous to walk under many parts of the steep cliffs because of rocks and falling snow. (*Photograph by the author*)

A cornice. Such a cornice can be extremely dangerous to anyone below it. Sooner or later it will fall. (*Photograph by the author*)

The archlike formation is another type of cornice. Some day it will fall. Such cornices and places below them are also to be avoided. (*Photograph by the author*)

Try to keep a steady pace for the next hour. On Mount Massive you will probably do a little scrambling—that is, climbing with hands and feet up a few large ledges. You may take a naturalist's stop and photograph a pool of water surrounded by wildflowers. You may take pictures of huge icicles eight or nine feet tall hanging down from boulders. You may see game: ptarmigans, marmots, even Rocky Mountain sheep. Huge vistas will open up to the east. On the horizon you will see endless snow-capped peaks.

Be careful of thirst. The dry air and wind can dehydrate you. Even a slight dehydration can slow you down terribly. A good drink of tea or water may give you more energy than a long rest.

Many beginners are surprised at how slowly they will be moving after gaining an elevation of 13,000 feet above sea level. It is such a new and uncanny experience that

This peak provides a good example of a route-finding problem. Some routes to the top of the peak would be difficult and call for expert climbing knowledge. However, there is a rather easy, though complicated route to the top, which is marked with a dotted line. Note that the route avoids the base of any steep cliffs. It also follows a rise; thus snow sliding downhill would not avalanche on any climbers. Climbers would have to test the last big snow field to see how conditions are. If they proved difficult, the climbers no doubt could discover a safe way of getting over to the rocks on the last visible rocky ridge of the peak. (*Photograph by the author*)

it can make you want to give up. It is known that a lack of oxygen cuts down a person's will power. Most climbers find the last thousand feet of a climb almost unbearable.

Mount Massive, luckily, does not wear you out with numerous false summits. On some peaks, especially where you are climbing a ridge, you look up and see the summit of the peak, but on arriving there, you realize it is not the summit but only a shoulder on the ridge. I recall going up Mount La Plata, 14,340 feet high. There were several false summits. Oddly enough, I misguessed the true summit. Until the last moment I was sure it was just another false summit.

On the summit of a peak of any importance you will usually see a big pile of rocks, called a cairn. In it there should be a pipe (in the good old days they were brass!) with screw tops at both ends. If you unscrew the top, inside you should find a register placed there by the Colorado Mountain Club. Before signing it, it is usually fun to read who has been on the mountain before you. Occasionally one comes across interesting notes: such as "Herman Potschcry—Jan. 15th, lone ascent temperature 42 degrees below zero. High winds. Almost did not make it."

After signing it, take out your notebook with your list of peaks visible from the summit. Since you have preplanned it all, you can quickly take bearings on them with your compass. Be sure that you do not have metal, such as your ice axe head, near the compass, as it will throw off the reading. Once I watched someone carefully rest his compass on top of the ice axe head to hold the compass steady.

Do not forget to take pictures. If the camera has settings, think carefully about them. High altitude and exhaustion can cause mistakes to be made very easily.

Mountain climbing accidents occur with more frequency when people are walking back after a climb. You are more tired. On a trail down you can easily twist a knee. All downhill trails are hard on the knees.

If you go down a scree slope, be sure to dig your heels into it on the way down. Do not take any short cuts down steep slopes or get off the trail.

On the way down, keep your camera handy. Some

people put their cameras away after the summit photographs.

It might be that you arrive at the summit in the very late afternoon, though you should not plan it that way. If you see that you are going to be camping out for another night, at least try to make it to timberline. Trees give you shelter from the wind, and they provide fuel for a campfire. Forests are not the safest places during a night thunderstorm, but they are much safer than areas above timberline.

13

Maps and How to Use Them

Mountain climbers need to know how to use topographic maps. These show in detail such surface features as hills, mountains, ridges, cliffs, and valleys. U.S. government topographic maps show the elevation of the land by means of contour lines. These are lines which connect all points of equal elevation. But what does this really mean?

Let us consider what a contour line would look like in reality. We could, for example, take an Egyptian pyramid, and think of it as sort of an ideal hill. It is obvious that if the pyramid is forty-eight feet high, there must be a point on it twenty feet above the ground. No matter how you climbed the pyramid, you would get to a place on it which was exactly twenty feet in elevation. The same, though, would be true for anyone climbing it any other place. In fact, there would be many points on it twenty feet in elevation.

Thus, you could very easily draw a line completely around the pyramid which was twenty feet in elevation. That would be a contour line. Moreover, you could repeat the process and mark lines every twenty feet in elevation up the pyramid. Thus, you would have contours for 20 feet, 40 feet, 60 feet, 80 feet, and so on. If you climbed such a pyramid and counted the contour lines as you went up, you could tell exactly what your elevation was any time you stood on a given contour line. Not only that, you could guess your elevation with a fair degree of accuracy between them. If, for example, you were standing between the 80-foot and the 100-foot contour lines, you would obviously be at a greater elevation than 80 feet but less than 100 feet. If you felt you were ap-

Contour lines drawn on a pyramid. Note how the lines change as you look more and more down onto the pyramid. From straight above, the lines would be like those printed on a topographic map. You can see how such lines indicate altitudes and the shape of an object. (*Photographs by the author*)

proximately halfway between them, you could say that you were at an elevation of 90 feet. If you felt you were three fourths of the way to the 100-foot contour mark, you could guess with some accuracy that you were at an elevation of 95 feet.

In reality, of course, the pyramids do not have contour lines marked on them and neither do hills. However, topographic maps show all hills as though they did have contour lines. Many government topographic maps have 40-foot contours marked on them. Thus, in counting contours up a mountain, as seen on a map, you would count from the base, 40, 80, 120, 160 feet, and so on. With the aid of the contours you can find the elevation of any given place on a topographical map.

In looking at such a map you will find many elevations of the contours marked. The contour line will be broken and in a space will be marked the contour elevation. It will look, perhaps, like this: ---- 4,000 ----. This means, of course, that that line is a contour line which is 4,000 feet above sea level. (On some maps, especially those used in foreign countries, 4,000 would refer to meters instead of feet.) The elevations of the tops of hills and summits of mountains are frequently given. An × is marked on the map and next to it is printed the elevation.

Moreover, there are bench marks indicated on the maps. A bench mark is a pipe placed in the ground on top of which is a metal plate with the elevation engraved on it. It is marked on the map as, for instance, × B.M. 3,569. Given all of those various elevations, it is easy to find the elevation of a given contour line. So you can see that one of the great advantages of a contour map is that you can find, with reasonable accuracy, the elevation of any place on it.

Another and equally great advantage of a topographic map marked with contour lines is that you can determine the lay of the land from it. In fact, with a topographic map you can visualize what the scenery of a given place will look like before ever visiting it. To help understand how this could be done, let us once more think of an Egyptian pyramid marked with contour lines. Egyptian pyramids were built with four sides. Imagine you are above a pyramid and looking straight down on it. It is obvious that the contour lines would all be in the form

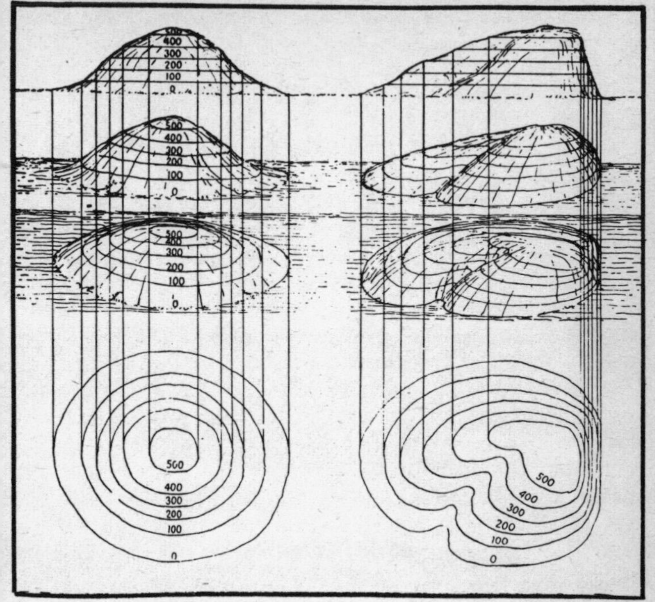

Mountain contours. Note how the contours show not only the elevations but the steepness of the slopes and shape of the mountains as well. (*After A. K. Lobeck*)

of squares. First you would see a large square, and in it a slightly smaller one, and in that another, and so on. If you saw such lines on a map, you would know that the map was indicating an Egyptian-type pyramid.

Let us consider some other possibilities. If the Egyptians had made three-sided pyramids, all the contours would be triangles. If they had built cones instead of pyramids all the contours would be circles.

In this way, the shape of the contour lines indicate the shape of a mountain or hill. A crescent-shaped mountain will have crescent-shaped contours. A four-sided mountain, which would not be a rarity, would have roughly square or rectangular-shaped contours. A dome or cone-shaped mountain, as, for example, a volcanic cone, would have roughly circular contours. For a mountain climber this is very important to know. Quite often when you are in a wilderness region, you will see many

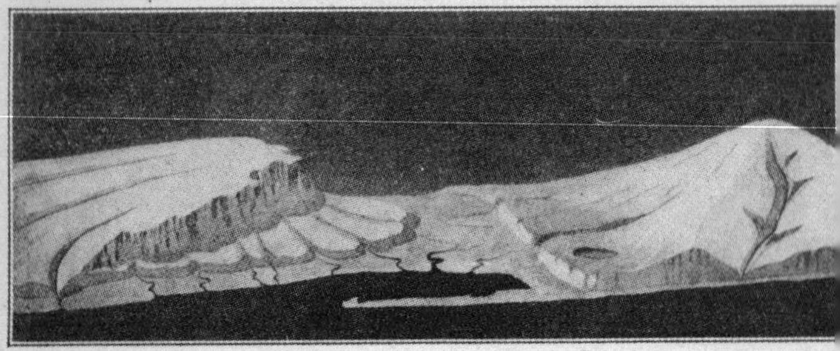

The same landscape shown on a topographic map and as it would look in reality. (*Courtesy U. S. Geologic Survey*)

mountain peaks around you. You may not know which is which. However, on looking at your topographic map, you might see that one particular peak is roughly triangular in shape. You notice that no other peak nearby has that shape. You look about, and sure enough, there is a peak with three sides.

Of course, contour maps do not simply show the shapes of peaks. They show river and stream courses. If you do not know exactly where you are, you can look at a topographic map and also at the streams near you. You might find that in the region near you there is only one place where three streams meet. If you see three streams meeting, you will know your location.

Contour maps are very helpful in determining the steepness of various slopes. Let us again see how this could be done by using an artificial example. This time we can pretend that we have a ladder. If we place it against a wall so that the base of it is far from the wall, the ladder is not too steep. If you looked straight down on such a ladder, you would see that the rungs are at a given distance from each other. Now if you pushed the base of the ladder closer and closer to the wall, the ladder would be steeper. At the same time the rungs of the ladder as seen from above would get closer and closer together. When the ladder was straight up and down the rungs would merge.

The rungs of a ladder are the same as contour lines, and thus it is evident that steep slopes have contour lines which are closer together. Gentler slopes have contour lines which are much farther apart. A perfectly flat area will have no contour lines.

By looking at contour lines, it is very easy to compare the steepness of one slope with that of another. You can also tell the exact steepness of a slope.

Let us say that you see a cliff and find on the map that it is a mile from the base of it to the top, or 5,280 feet. Place a ruler between those two points and count the number of contours. Let us say that you count off 132 contours. If the contours represent 40 feet in elevation, the cliff is a mile high, or 5,280 feet high. The slope of the cliff is 45 degrees. If on the other hand you count 264 contours in the same distance, the cliff would be much steeper, namely 63°27′. To determine that, all you have to do is divide the vertical height of the cliff by the horizontal distance, which gives you the tangent. Then look that number up in a table of tangents in a mathematics book. From that, you can obtain the exact angle of the cliff. Even if you do not go to all that trouble, you can easily compare cliffs, which can be a very handy thing to do.

Many times you will want to know the relative positions of two places on a map. Let us say that you wish to know the direction of Mount Adams from the junction of State Highway 7 and County Road 9.

There are two ways of doing it. One way is to orient the map. This means to get the map lined up in a north-south direction. All maps show, someplace, an arrow pointing north. The arrow will point toward true north, not magnetic north; but many maps show an arrow for magnetic north as well.

Take a compass and place it on the magnetic north arrow and move the map with the compass on it until the needle and arrow line up. Of course, in doing so, be sure that you do it on something flat. Also be sure no metal is near. Any barbed-wire fences? An ice axe? An automobile?

When the magnetic north arrow and the compass are lined up, the map is oriented. Next, place the compass center over the road junction and read the direction to Mount Adams. On the side of the compass circle will be bearings in degrees going from 0 degrees at north to 90 degrees east, 180 degrees south, 270 degrees west, and 360 degrees north again. Reading from the center of the compass to Mount Adams you will see the degrees. If it is difficult to sight it, place a ruler or the edge of a piece of paper from the compass center to Mount Adams. Most compasses today are designed with a transparent base so that it is easy to do all of that. If the compass does not have a transparent base, then draw, with a straight edge, a line from Mount Adams to the road junction and place the center of the compass on the line and again read the direction.

What do you do if the map does not have a magnetic north arrow? Some do not. If that is the case, look on the map and see if the magnetic declination for the region is listed. The compass needle does not point toward the truth north but a few degrees away from it toward the magnetic north pole. The declination might be, for instance, 15° E, as it is in some of the Rockies. That means the compass needle will point 15 degrees east of where true north is located. In that case, place the compass on the north arrow. When the compass needle is pointing 15 degrees east, the map is oriented.

The other way of getting a bearing between two places is to see if the edge of the map is such that it goes due north and south. More than ninety per cent of all maps are made that way. Draw a line between the road junction and Mount Adams. Extend the line to the edge of the map. The line will make an angle with the edge. Measure the angle with a protractor. Measure the angle from the north. This is usually the quickest, easiest, and most accurate way of getting a bearing.

If for some reason the map's edges do not line up in a north-south direction, just draw a straight line through the compass arrow marked on the map. Extend it across the map and use that line as you would the edge.

Once you know the bearing between two places, you can use your compass to get from one point to another. In the above instance you would know how to go from the road junction to the summit of Mount Adams. This would be particularly helpful to know if you had to pass through dense forests.

Let us say that you have found your bearing to be 45 degrees. Knowing that, you can walk to the mountain. All you need to do to start is hold the compass in your hand at the road junction and wait until the needle points toward north. Set the 0° mark due north. This is done according to the local magnetic variation. If, for example, it is 15 degrees east, the compass needle will be pointing toward 15°, and the 0° or true north will be correct. Next, sight over the center of the compass to the 45° mark. Look as far ahead as you can in that direction and pick out an object, such as a tree, a stump, a rock, or whatever. Walk directly toward it. When you get to it, stand at that object and repeat the whole process and once again walk 45 degrees. By going 45 degrees in a straight line from object to object, you will eventually get to the mountain.

Practice this before going on a trip in the wilds.

Every now and then you may be hiking on a large plateau or be in an area where you do not know your exact location. With a compass and map you can determine quite easily where you are if you know what some distant mountains are.

Let us say that you are on a large plateau, such as South Park, Colorado. You can see in the distance Pikes Peak, Bison Mountain, and Mount Lincoln, all of which you recognize and can positively identify. Take your map and orient it. Next, hold your compass so that the 0° mark is toward north. Sight to Pikes Peak. You find that it is on a bearing of 120 degrees. Then a line drawn from Pikes Peak on a bearing of 120 degrees will be going directly away from you, but if you extend it back in the opposite direction, it will pass through the point where you are located. So all you have to do is draw a line from Pikes Peak going 120 degrees and extend it right back across the map in your direction.

Next, sight Bison Mountain. It, you find, is 339 degrees. From it draw a line going in that direction, and once more extend the line both ways across the map. You'll notice that the two lines you have drawn cross each other. Do the same with a bearing to Mount Lincoln, which has a bearing of 304 degrees. Once more draw a line. If it were possible for your calculations to be absolutely accurate, it would meet the other two lines exactly at the point where they have already crossed each other. In actual fact, you will find there will be a small triangle where the three lines nearly meet. You will be in the middle of the triangle.

Using three distant objects like that will give you good results. If you use two objects and find their bearings, you can safely say that you are quite close to the place where the two lines cross, but not with such certainty.

Occasionally you must rely on one object. Let us say that you are in South Park and take a bearing on Pikes Peak and find that it is on a bearing of 90 degrees. Once more you can draw a line across the map and you will know that you are on that line. You can also estimate how close you are to the peak. For instance, you can realize that you are not within five miles of its summit. On the other hand you are not twenty miles away. Thus, on that one firm line, you are somewhere between five miles and twenty miles from the peak. Even with that information you can often determine where you are if you study the map. A stream, a road, an odd-looking hill may clue you into a much more exact location. Furthermore, if you know you are on a given fifteen-mile-long line, you might be able to name other peaks in the distance with certainty and use them to gain the other two bearings for an exact location.

It takes a little practice to use a compass and map quickly and easily. However, once you learn, you can find locations rapidly. In practicing all of this, you will note that it is important for a mountain climber to know the names of distant peaks. They always serve as beacons. When you go into any new territory, find out the names of major peaks. They are the handiest for determining locations. You can also use other topographical features such as lakes. Every lake has a distinct shape and is thus one of the easiest of all natural features to identify. In taking a bearing from a lake, use one end or a cape on its shore. Do not try to use the middle of a lake for a bearing, as it is difficult to determine the center of a lake.

Often you will want to know the name of a peak. The easiest way to do it is to find your exact location and take a compass bearing on it. On the map draw a line from where you are standing on that bearing and the line should go right through the peak.

Another way, using a topographic map, is, as we have seen, to look carefully at its shape and determine it from its contour lines.

If you ever happen to be lost but have a map and compass with you, you should not have too much trouble locating where you are.

If you happen to be lost near a trail or road, find out from your map which way they run. A road may go north to south, or southwest to northeast. When you discover the general direction of the road, head toward it. Go in a direction at right angles to the road.

For example, let us say you are near a north-south highway, and you know that you are to the west of it. Go due east. That is at right angles to the road and the shortest distance to it.

When you are lost, it is usually easiest to head for a road or trail. Once there you will probably meet someone. Even if you don't, at least you know where you are.

Topographic maps can help you determine your altitude with considerable accuracy. Because mountains erode in uneven shapes, they often have cliffs on them. Now from the contour map you can see where the top of the cliff is located and where the base of it is located, for the contour lines change. Even though you may not be on the cliff, you can tell rather easily if you are higher or lower than the base or the top of it. By carefully picking out many features and looking at contours, you can usually find several key points and use them as "altimeters." Actual barometric altimeters are frequently not as accurate. For one thing, even in the mountains barometric pressure can change. Once, near the summit of Mount Elbert, 14,433 feet above sea level, we got a reading of 16,000 feet with an expensive barometric altimeter. A low pressure storm was passing over the peak.

A topographic map can give you an exact elevation. However, who wants to pull out a map all the time? Quite often nature will provide rough keys to the altitude of a region.

Timberline is the place where trees no longer grow on a mountain. Above it the land is barren, though flowers and some shrubs do grow above the height. On a mountain timberline is a definite and unmistakable feature. The timberlines on mountains are not at the same elevation all over the world. For example, timberline is at sea level for most places around Hudson Bay in Canada. However, in Mexico it is above 14,000 feet. Thus, for different places, roughly following latitudes, timberline varies a great deal. Luckily for the climber, timberline in a given region varies very slightly; in Colorado it is around 12,500 feet. One of the most remarkable things to see is timberline on the west flank of Pikes Peak. It looks as though someone had taken a ruler and marked it off, it is so straight and even. By knowing the elevation of local timberlines, a climber should be able to make a guess of his elevation within a couple of hundred feet when he is standing at timberline.

Plants themselves can frequently be used as living altimeters. For example, foxtail pines live at high elevations and when you are in a grove of them, you know timberline is not too far away. Climbers can do very well with a knowledge of plants. Different types of vegetation indicate a great number of things: the elevation, the dryness of slopes, water seeps, and so forth.

Animals, too, live at various altitudes, but since they can move around, they are not reliable guides.

Quite frequently climbers will be on vertical cliffs. You can tell the height of a cliff by throwing a stone from it. Of course, when you use this method, you must be careful no one is below. On some cliffs you can simply drop a stone and it will go straight down to the bottom of the cliff. At other times, when the cliff is not absolutely perpendicular, you must throw the stone away from it. Throw it straight out, neither up nor down. Be careful. Do not lose your balance!

Once you drop or throw the stone, count in seconds how long it takes to hit the ground below. Take the number of seconds, square it, and multiply by 16 to get the distance in feet the stone fell. Thus if the stone falls 1 second, it has fallen 16 feet (1 × 1 × 16). If it falls 2 seconds, it has fallen 64 feet (2 × 2 × 16), and so on. The following chart will show you the distance it falls.

THE DISTANCE A STONE FALLS IN A GIVEN TIME

Number of Seconds	*Distance the Stone Falls*
1	16 feet
2	64 feet
3	144 feet
4	256 feet
5	400 feet
6	576 feet
7	784 feet
8	1024 feet
9	1296 feet
10	1600 feet
11	1936 feet
12	2304 feet
13	2704 feet
14	3136 feet
15	3600 feet

It is extremely difficult to determine distances in the mountains. The air is so thin and clear that distant objects almost always look much closer than they really are. People from the flatlands often think a peak some thirty miles away is only four or five miles away. It is also difficult for them to realize that you can sometimes see mountains which are over 150 miles away. But there is no real way to judge distance accurately from looking at a known object; even at best, the method is very rough.

There is one method, which is not often used, for determining distances, heights, and so forth. It is called the stadia method. It requires that you have a measuring tape with you. However, if you are studying the distances and heights of cliffs, the method can be useful, especially if you like mathematics.

Measure a companion's height from his belt to the top of his head. Let us say that it is three feet. Stand him in front of a distant cliff, which you know is 1,000 feet high. You back up and look at the top of his head and his belt. Keep backing until you reach a point where the top of his head is even with the cliff's top, and his belt is even with the bottom of the cliff. To find this point where both align at the same time, you will probably have to stoop somewhat to get your eyes at just the right level—depending on the height of the place you are standing in relation to the bottom of the cliff. If you are approximately level with the bottom of the cliff, then your eyes should be at about the level of your companion's belt. If you are below the bottom of the cliff, then your eyes must be even lower than his belt; if you are higher, then higher. (If you should be higher than the *top* of the cliff—say, standing across a valley on another cliff or peak—then your eyes will have to be higher than your companion's head. You might find it helpful to have him kneeling; but he should keep the upper part of his body straight up and down.)

Let us say that you find this point when you are thirty feet from your companion. Then the ratio between the height you measured on his body, three feet, and your distance from him is 3:30, or 1:10. The ratio of the height of the cliff to its distance from you will be the same, 1:10. Since you know the cliff is 1,000 feet high, that means that it is 10,000 feet away.

The stadia method can also be used to determine heights. Let us say you are looking at a cliff and most of it looks easy, but there is a section which looks difficult. There is a smooth slab of rock. How tall is the slab of rock? Determine your distance from the cliff, using a good map. If necessary, move to a spot you can locate precisely on the map. Let us say that you are 1,000 feet from the slab. Next, hold up a ruler and look at the slab of rock and sight the ruler along it. You hold a ruler two feet from your eye. This distance can be measured by a companion. You note that the slab covers one-half inch. Since the ruler is two feet, or 24 inches, from your eye, you have a ratio of ½:24, or 1:48. The cliff is 1,000 feet away; thus the height of the slab of rock is about 1/48 of that distance, or 20.8 feet. You can obtain quite good results using the stadia method.

A few binoculars have "stadia" markings in them. These can be accurate for all practical purposes.

The easiest way to find direction is to use a compass. But you can find an approximate south with your watch if it is accurate. Here is how you do it. Point the hour hand of your watch toward the sun. Halfway between it and the numeral twelve on the watch's face will be toward the south. Thus, if the hour hand is at ten, south is halfway between it and the twelve, or opposite the numeral eleven.

At night you can discover where north is if you look up in the sky and see the Big Dipper, a constellation of seven stars. The two stars that form the outer edge of the

Mintaka

The constellation Orion. The three stars close together are called the belt. The upper right star of the belt is Mintaka. All year long it rises due east and sets due west.

dipper point toward the North Star. This star, for all practical purposes, is close to being due north.

If you know the constellation Orion, you can use it to tell where due east and west are. The star at the upper right end of Orion's belt is called Mintaka (or Delta Orionis). It is directly over the earth's equator and because of this it always rises due east and sets due west as seen from any place on earth.

As mentioned, it is a good idea to write down the rising time and setting time of the sun for the days you are going climbing. The sun passes due south at the midpoint between its rising and setting times. If you also write down the rising and setting times for planets, you can use them the same way.

Sometimes on a trip a watch will wind down and stop. It is handy to know what time it is so that you can set up camp at a given time and get all prepared before dark. In fact, there are several other reasons for wanting to know the time.

You can use some of the above information to help you set a watch. The rising and setting times of the sun and planets would obviously help. If you have a clear view of a horizon, you can set your watch within a few minutes by watching them as they rise or set.

14

Route Finding

Mountain climbing is a sport which often takes a person into trackless wilderness regions. In such a place you are on your own. You will need to know how to get from the end of a trail to the mountain you desire to climb. That calls for route finding.

Route finding is a two-part activity. You must know what to avoid on one hand and what to seek on the other. For route finding you will, of course, need a compass and a good map, but neither can answer certain questions: where there are fallen timber, snowdrifts, scree slopes, and so on. Route finding also calls for a certain ability to "read" the landscape. This is developed, more or less, through a knowledge of geology and through experience.

Let us start with those things a climber would want to avoid. Avoid fallen timber. It is extremely difficult to walk through a forest where many trees have fallen. The logs and branches on the ground are a barrier. Logs which can break or roll are dangerous, as you can easily hurt yourself. Moreover, all the branches sticking this way and that can be a constant threat to your eyes.

You cannot always tell from a distance whether or not a forest will have broken timber. However, it is obvious that a thickly forested area may have it, whereas barren or grassy areas will not. Unless you know that a forest is free of undergrowth—as many are—it is often best to avoid it.

The next thing to avoid is a deep snowdrift. If it is on rather level ground, it will not present dangers, but it can nevertheless be exhausting to walk on if the snow is soft.

There is no exact way of telling where you will find snowdrifts. However, there are some rules of thumb. Mountainous regions are often windy. The wind will blow snow away from some places and into others, causing drifts to accumulate. If you are in an area where winter storms come from the west, then you can expect that western slopes, slightly below north-south ridges, will be clearest of snow. The west wind will blow it up and over the ridge. Conversely, on the eastern slopes snowdrifts will grow. Snowdrifts often occur in hollows and depressions, but not on rises of land. Snow will be blown across barren lands, but will build up in a grove of trees, or around large boulders. Areas exposed to the sun will be freer of snow than areas which are shady, such as deep forests, north-facing slopes, and so on.

Choosing a route through regions where there are numerous snowdrifts can be tricky. Of course, try to avoid them. Secondly, head for rises and ridges. Sometimes snowdrifts in the sun will be soft, whereas those in a shaded area can be hard enough to walk on top. The worst snow is that in forests, for you cannot tell what is under your feet. Thus, snow over barren ground is safer than that over trees or boulders.

Thickets are difficult to walk through. The branches of the bushes are always pushing against you. On a steep slope they can be miserable, as they keep you off balance.

In the summertime, thickets present another problem. Often they harbor ticks or insects. Ticks carry several diseases such as Rocky Mountain spotted fever. Flies and mosquitoes also stay around thickets.

Boulder fields are also difficult to cross. Boulders can come in all shapes and sizes from basketball-sized rocks to immense ones as big as a house. If boulders are large enough so that they do not move when you walk over them, boulder fields are not too dangerous—only time consuming. In some fields you can leap from boulder to boulder, which is exhausting, or you can "climb" them, which is also exhausting and even slower.

Dangerous boulder fields are those in which the boulders rock back and forth when you step on them. If at all possible, avoid such a place. Often in such a place there are secure boulders amidst wobbly ones. You can leap from insecure boulder to secure boulder as rapidly and gracefully as possible and rest on the secure ones. But you must be very careful.

The worst boulder fields are those on a relatively steep slope. When you step on the boulders, many move at once downhill. Do not cross such a place. If you find yourself on such a slope get off it by going back to known solid ground. Do not go down it, as the further down the slope you go, the more boulders there are which could roll downward toward you.

Many slopes can be covered with rocks smaller than boulders. Such slopes can also be unstable. When you walk on them, they, too, can give and slide. If the rocks are small enough, they will not be as dangerous as boulder fields. Even so, they are tiring to cross and never give you a firm footing. Most mountains and cliffs have lower slopes covered with such loose materials, called talus if it is composed of broken rocks and scree if it is made up of rocks gravel size or smaller. Try to see where they are located. They are usually at the base of gullies, large cliffs, and the slopes of canyons. The base of ridges are usually freer of them.

Avoid slippery slopes, such as those covered with leaves, pine needles, and grass. Grassy slopes, especially, can be dangerous. Mountain boots and rubber soles are not built for grassy areas and will not hold well on such slopes.

Boggy areas are not dangerous. On the other hand, who wants to walk through muck? The upper edges of lakes often have bogs. Occasionally you find them near streams. If the weather is cold enough, do not neglect a bog. If it is frozen with solid ice, you can easily cross over it.

Lakes and streams, of course, form barriers. Be very careful in crossing any stream. Many mountain streams flow very rapidly, and if the stream is deeper than your knees, it can drag you downhill. Even in midwinter, streams usually will not freeze over. Lakes, though, will freeze, and if the ice is thick enough—about five inches—it is safe to walk across. Of course you can test the ice with your ice axe, cutting through the ice to check it.

Glaciers are difficult to cross and require extra precautions. Do not cross one unless you are fully prepared and can rescue a person who falls in a crevasse. If possible, avoid glaciers.

In choosing a route, try not to cross ridges. It is best

to walk parallel to them. It takes time and effort to go up and down ridges.

You know that it takes more energy to go up a steep slope than a gentle slope. In choosing a route try to plan it so that the party goes up moderate slopes, even if it calls for a zigzag route up the side of a mountain. In fact, most routes are in the form of a zigzag. Try to keep away from steep areas. On the other hand, do not choose a slope so gentle that the distance from the base of the mountain to the summit is made longer than it needs to be.

Now that we have seen what not to choose, let us see what you should choose. First, you should try to find a route that is not blind. Look for a route which has the best views. That way you can see the topography ahead and behind. High, barren ground affords one of the best routes, especially if you can see for miles around.

Choose a route along ridges, if possible. They are high and often are clear of forests. Often they lead right to the mountain you are heading toward. Unfortunately, many ridges are uneven and you must go up and down all the time on them. If so, it may very well be best to traverse a ridge, that is, go along the edge of it about halfway between a valley and the crest.

Many streams have trails along them. Generally, routes along streams are the best to take. On the other hand, they can also be the very worst. If a stream moves through a V canyon and there are no trails, then it's a bad choice. Also, during early summer many stream trails are blocked with snowdrifts because the sun cannot reach down between the high walls. Thus, a stream trail might be great in August but be impossible the first week of June.

In determining a stream trail, find out if any local people can give you information about it. If not, check the trail for recent footprints. If you do not see any hikers' footprints, think for a minute. Is the trail blocked? Or is it just that no one has been on it? The only really reliable thing is to see footprints going in with none coming out. That shows someone went in and probably continued for the full length of the trail, indicating that the trail is okay.

The sides of canyons often are good choices, especially if the slope faces southward. The sun will be nice and warm early in the season, and will free the slopes of snow. Moreover, the sunlight often makes a south-facing slope the driest of all, preventing thick forests and keeping the place rather barren.

If you choose a slope to traverse, look at your topographic map to see that it does not get steeper later on. Many people have been walking along nice slopes only to find out after an hour's hike that the nice slope changes to cliffs.

In choosing routes, it is helpful to know that some forests are more dense than others. Piñon pine–juniper forests are almost never dense. Aspen forests are usually open. Spruce and some types of pines, such as white pine, can make dense forests. In general, forests are less dense on ridges than in hollows and valleys.

Geologically speaking, areas eroded by glaciers are usually more difficult to cross than places eroded by streams. Lava fields are the most difficult areas to cross. Lava forms sharp ridges, and it can cut boots to ribbons. Avoid areas of "rotten rock," meaning places where rocks break easily. Solid rock is better.

In choosing a route, try to go where there is a plentiful supply of drinkable water. Be sure that you get to enough streams and lakes. Do not trust the "spring marks" on topographic maps. Springs have a bad habit of drying up. Worse, some springs have undrinkable water. They may be polluted, too salty, or in a few cases contain poisons such as arsenic, which, by the way, comes from natural sources.

In choosing a route across snow, try to get on firm snow. Snow which looks grainy at a distance is usually not firm. Firm snow often has a slick-looking glaze in sunlight. However, such a glaze may indicate only a thin crust. On the other hand, avoid actual ice. Quite often snow in the shadow of a cliff will be different from that in the sunlight.

Snow can sometimes melt, harden again, melt once more, and so on. This can give it a wavy surface. At times it can even produce weird formations. You may encounter them. The snow may melt and refreeze in such a way that tall, thin mounds form, almost as high as human forms. Because someone once thought they looked like bowed-down praying men or women, they are called "penitentes." Once, coming off of Mount Whitney, a friend and I had a nightmarish time crossing a field of them. There was not one level place to stand. For about an hour we slipped and slid among them.

In route finding one must watch out for cornices. These are piles of snow which overhang a slope. Almost all cornices form on the edges of ridges. They are formed as snow blown upward along a ridge begins to sweep over it on the lee side. Particles of snow stick to each other and after a while they protrude outward. Cornices can be very large indeed, weighing hundreds, even thousands of tons. Ice and snow frozen together can make them "stick" to a cliff or the lip of a ridge. However, all cornices fall at some time or other. Either they become too big and heavy for the frozen sections to hold, or the weather warms up, melting the ice. When cornices fall, they can be extremely dangerous, sweeping everything in their path. Cornices can easily slide a mile down a slope and even farther at times. Be sure to look for them. If you see one, decide where it will fall and consider what its path will be, and stay away from any possible danger. Be sure not to try to outguess a cornice. It is in the nature of it that it can go at any time, night or day.

Avalanches can be even more dangerous since so much snow is involved. They can take down trees and bury whole villages. Most avalanches occur where old ones have already taken place. Often you can see where there has been an old avalanche. If you see slopes with no trees, you can pretty well guess that old avalanches wiped them out. Most avalanches occur in gullies, which are depressed areas of a slope. They can also start on open but even slopes. Quite often they can start on slopes which are not steep. Really steep slopes shed snow and never give it a chance to get deep enough for a big avalanche. As you would guess, avalanches occur least on bulging slopes or on ridges. In fact, ridges are the only places which are almost free of them.

Avalanches can travel a long way, covering a mile in a few seconds. It seems incredible, but the snow in a falling avalanche compresses air and the snow rides down the mountainside on a cushion of air. The compressed air can blast things down. Moreover, an avalanche can cross a valley and ride up the opposite slope for a distance.

Avalanches occur most often after a heavy snowfall. They also occur when the sun is shining on a slope. Though avalanches can happen at any time that there is heavy snow on the ground, they occur less frequently at night, especially in the predawn hours. At that time the snow and rocks are cool and more or less the same temperature. Moreover, the snow is frozen and there is no running water under it. Many climbers get as far up a mountain as they can before the sun rises, to avoid avalanche dangers. The worst season for avalanches is during the springtime, with winter a close second. By midsummer, avalanche dangers have mainly passed, and autumn is the time when they occur least of all.

Rock falls are also a danger. Do not choose a route which takes you under high cliffs, especially those which have loose rock. Deep gullies can be very dangerous. People who have never been in mountainous regions can hardly believe how much rock actually falls. Once I was with a friend at Lawn Lake in Rocky Mountain National Park during early June—a bad time to be there. All day long we could hear rocks falling from the mountains around us. Some rocks were huge, as big as semitrailer trucks. We did not have to be told that many of the cliffs there were dangerous.

Rocks fall for two reasons. During the day, water may get between a rock and the mountain's side. At night the water will freeze. Ice expands and pushes the rock outward. At the same time, it often holds the rock. When the sun rises once again, the ice holding the rock melts and the rock falls. As with avalanches, the predawn hours are the safest. At that time the ice is still holding the rocks to the mountainside. Slopes with the sun shining on them are the worst. In general, the seasons for rock falls are the same as for avalanches, except that heavy rains can also cause rocks to fall. Rocks do not travel as far as avalanches, although every now and then one will roll quite a distance.

The safest places in terms of rock falls are areas away from cliffs, areas above cliffs, and ridges. If you must cross a place where rocks do fall, cross it as quickly as possible. If you are ever in a spot where rocks are falling toward you, try to get behind a boulder. If you are on a steep cliff, get close to the cliff. Rocks hitting the side of steep cliffs usually bounce away from the cliff; so being in close helps.

If there is no way to your mountain except by going over avalanche and rock-fall areas and there is a danger, do it before dawn. On the way back, cross the areas again after the sun has set behind some peaks and the areas are in shadow. At high altitudes, places freeze up rapidly after the sun moves away.

In some mountainous regions, especially in the American Southwest, rains can be violent. A cloudburst can turn a dry stream bed into a raging torrent in half an hour. In planning a route, do not walk up dry stream beds between perpendicular walls when there is the slightest danger of heavy rains even thirty miles away. Summertime is the worst time for rains. The colder the weather, the less chance of a flash flood. Higher up in mountainous regions, streams can become swollen, blocking your retreat. Plan the route so that you will not be trapped.

15

Mountain Climate and Weather

The climate in mountains around the world varies, but there are also many similarities. All mountains rise into thinner air. Air holds heat, and the thinner it is, the less it can hold. Thus, the higher in elevation a mountain is, the cooler it will be.

As you climb a high peak, you notice how much cooler it gets. Usually there is a drop of about 3.3 degrees in temperature per thousand feet. This is known technically as the lapse rate. Dry air cools more per thousand feet than damp air. Sometimes the lapse rate can be as high as 5.4 degrees per thousand feet. It is this fact which explains why tropical mountains have snow on them. Thus, a South American town at sea level may be as warm as 80° F, and a peak 20,000 feet high nearby may have a temperature at its summit of only 20 degrees.

Many snow-capped peaks are on the equator itself. A great many mountains never have any summer weather. Their climates, in many ways, are comparable to Arctic climates. In fact, many Arctic animals and plants live on mountain peaks in states like California and Colorado.

Most mountains have heavier rainfall than the lands surrounding them. The reason is that moist warm air moving across the lowlands is forced upward as it meets the mountains. As the warm air rises to move over the mountains, it cools. Once that happens, water condenses and it starts to rain. Some of the wettest places on earth are in mountains. The Hawaiian mountains have had more than 300 inches of rain in a year. The heaviest recorded snowfalls have been in the Sierra Nevada of California, where over 100 feet of snow has fallen in a winter.

A climber approaching the summit of Mount Logan, 19,850 feet above sea level, Canada's highest peak. Behind him, threatening dark clouds are gathering. Most mountains have treacherous weather conditions. (*Courtesy the American Alpine Club*)

Not all mountains are wet, however. Some are drier than the lowlands. Let us consider two mountain ranges, one east of the other. Let us say that almost all rainstorms and damp air come from the west. These hit the first range of mountains and a heavy rainfall takes place. The wind continues, but is now much drier. The second range to the east may experience very dry weather.

The sun shining on mountains is so bright and the temperature at which water boils so much less than at sea level that water evaporates more rapidly. After a rain, the puddles can disappear very fast. On dry days, mountain air can be very, very dry, causing your lips to crack.

Mountains are among the windiest places on earth. It is very rare to climb a mountain on a still, calm day. It is far more frequent to meet winds which are 40 miles an hour and higher. Several times I have been climbing in the Rockies when the wind has hit more than 100 miles per hour. The highest winds ever recorded on earth were in the White Mountains of New Hampshire. Winds there hit 231 miles per hour.

In general, mountain weather is influenced by the same weather conditions which affect the surrounding area.

When you are located in a cold air mass, the weather is usually still, often dry, and either cool or cold. The skies are usually clear. The barometer readings are higher than normal. Some of the best climbing weather is during the time when a cold air mass is over the mountains. On a weather map you can spot cold air masses, as they are usually marked as highs. They are circular in shape, and government meteorologists place an H in the middle of them. In the northern hemisphere, winds rotate clockwise around a cold air mass.

Warm air masses are known as lows. When you are in the middle of a warm air mass at sea level, the temperature is warm or hot, but not in the high mountains. Since warm air masses have within them a great deal of moisture, you can frequently expect rain, especially in mountainous regions. The rocks and snow fields of a mountain can cool the temperature of such warm, moist air masses, causing local rains. In general, climbs during a time when a warm air mass is centered overhead are riskier than those during cold air masses.

Rain or snow frequently falls when a warm air mass meets a cold one, for the moist air in it is cooled and the water vapor condenses. When a cold air mass moves into a warm air mass, the cold air rises and lifts the warm air, cooling it very rapidly. At times like that, there can be a thunderstorm. In the winter a cold air mass moving into a warm one can produce a blizzard.

Warm air masses can move toward cold air masses. When they do so, they slide up over the cooled heavier air. Again the warm air is cooled, and rain falls, but not so violently. Snow can also fall and in fact become quite deep.

Sometimes when climbing you will be miles from any local newspaper with its weather report. However, you can sometimes tell when air masses are meeting. Cold air masses come in from the north, northwest, or northeast. Usually, large cumulus clouds, which look like fluffy cotton balls, will form rapidly and build up into thunderheads. A heavy rain is due in a matter of hours. When you see such a change, retreat from a high mountain peak, or if you are climbing a cliff, get down.

A warm front moving into a cold front is quite different. The first sign is often high feathery-looking clouds coming from the south, southwest, or southeast. They are followed by thickening clouds, usually stratus clouds, which lie in layers across the sky. They get lower, and rain or snow falls. Weather develops more slowly with such conditions, and you often have about six hours to prepare for the weather change.

From a local weather map you can determine where fronts are, and decide the best time to climb in the mountains. Do not climb when two fronts are about to meet. A climb done while a cold air mass is centered overhead is probably best.

Clear cold is not a threat to climbers, but they should be dressed for it.

Lightning is a distinct threat. All things being equal, lightning hits high places and skips over low places. Thus, a high summit is one of the most dangerous of all places to be. High ridges are also extremely dangerous. If on either, get off as quickly as possible. Some peaks are hit time and time again, even in the same storm.

Lightning is not grounded immediately, meaning it does not go underground right away. It tends to follow ruts and gullies downhill. This is why overhanging rock may not be such a protection, for the lightning tends to move into hollows once it hits above on a ridge. It can go down a gully and if the overhanging rock is near it, the lightning can move in under it. Once off a summit or ridge, you are safer on a slope away from gullies, hollows, and so on.

If you are in a lightning storm and are in a large meadow, it is best to lie down. Do not seek shelter under a lone tree or even a small group of trees.

All climbers should, of course, recognize the weather signs of an approaching thunderstorm. Thunder and lightning storms are not very different in the mountains from those found any place else. Familiarize yourself with the shape of thunderheads, the quick buildup of clouds, and the gusts of wind which precede a storm. Remember that most thunderstorms occur in the afternoon.

Climbers will sometimes see strange phenomena connected with static electricity. Sometimes on cold days the air in mountainous regions becomes extremely dry. At such times there are displays of static electricity, which can be quite dramatic.

One time I was on the summit of Pikes Peak on New Year's Eve and I was roped up with other climbers. Glowing ribbons of electricity zigzagged along the rope. I recall a few minutes later seeing someone whose parka was lit. I told him I thought he had left a flashlight on in his pocket, for that is what the glow looked like. He looked down and said, "How can there be a light on?" He began searching the parka, and then we both realized that it was glowing from static electricity.

Static electricity is not harmful on dry days; but if it occurs on a wet day, it can be considered a prelude to a lightning storm, and thus potentially dangerous.

Next to a lightning storm, a blizzard is probably the most dangerous weather condition. Blizzards in high mountains can be fierce. First of all, more snow will fall than in plains blizzards. Secondly, the wind speeds can be much higher. Thirdly, the wind can frequently rip away the crust of old snow and begin to circulate the dry powdery snow under it. Thus, the air is filled not only with falling snow but with old snow being circulated once more. In fact, there are frequent "ground blizzards" in which no snow is actually falling at all, just snow on the ground loosened by the wind.

In a blizzard climbers are in an immediate danger. Visibility drops to zero at times. You sometimes have extreme difficulty walking into the wind and wind-blown snow. If you have no goggles on (which would be a mistake), the snow will stab you in the eyes. If you have on your goggles, the snow can quickly plaster them. At the same time, the wind-chill factor increases, the deepening snow is difficult to walk in, and footprints and old trail marks can disappear in a few minutes.

If climbers are caught in a blizzard, they must immediately rope up, even if the ground is rather level, and stay roped up. The leader should try as quickly as possible to determine what route should be taken. It is frequently a mistake to go into the wind, even if that is the shortest route back to safety. Sometimes the best route is a longer one, in which the party will walk with the wind. Of course, it all depends on several factors, but in general it is far better to walk with the wind.

During a blizzard the party must also avoid cliffs and so on. Snow usually piles up in hollows and depressions, but is blown off ridges, so it is usually best during a blizzard to stay on ridges and high ground. A blizzard above timberline is worse than one below timberline. At times it may be wisest to head for timberline if you are above it, and seek out the protective cover of trees. They can and do block the wind. In a dense forest you will be far safer than on barren wind-swept slopes. Thus, the party must make some choices. A few moments spent considering them, after tying up, is worthwhile. The pros and cons of all choices should be aired.

Fortunately for the climber, it almost always takes a few hours for a true blizzard to develop. The signs are much the same as they are for those which develop any place else. Climbers must keep an eye out for them. If in doubt about the weather—retreat. A blizzard is too much to fool with, and even if the chances of one do not seem too great, it is wisest to get off the mountain.

The "white-out" is another odd phenomenon. Sometimes climbers will be in mountains completely covered with snow. The sky will be overcast and also white. During such times a white-out may occur. This means that everything looks white. There are no shadows or skyline. Once shadows disappear, you have a real problem telling where there are steep slopes, hollows, and so on. The danger in a white-out is that you can walk right onto a steep slope and not realize it until too late. Luckily, the very snow which causes a white-out can be of some help. If you do not know exactly how steep a slope is, you can make a snowball and toss it on the ground. If the snowball suddenly rolls off at a fast clip, you will know that there is a steep slope there.

During white-outs, you must be extra careful of snow blindness. Be sure that your eyes are protected.

White-outs can cause you to suffer from a psychological malaise. During a white-out, some people feel depressed or "empty." Eskimos who are familiar with this phenomenon often mention strange feelings they have during such times. The reason is that we are so used to focusing on things with our eyes and thinking about what we are looking at, that when there is virtually nothing to see, our minds become disoriented. This is especially true for the leader, who is walking along into "nothing." The people following can at least look at each other. Thus, the best thing to do is switch leaders every now and then. The climber is not faced with days of white-outs as an Arctic explorer might be. Rarely does he have to suffer more than a few days of it. He will soon return to a normal world, and the empty feeling will pass.

In mountainous regions there is an uneven cooling of peaks and valleys, which a climber should know about. Rocks radiate heat. Quite often at night, the rocks of high peaks will cool down very rapidly after sunset, so the air touching them becomes very cold. This air is heavy and starts to move downhill. Like water it flows into valleys. Right after sunset you will frequently notice that a cold breeze is moving downhill along the valley. Thus, it is not best to camp right on the floor of a mountain valley, but better to choose a place a couple hundred feet above it.

In the morning a similar effect can take place. Cold air gets chilled all night around the peaks. When the sunlight hits the peaks, the rocks will warm up rather quickly. The air near them will expand. As it does, it pushes away the remaining cold air, which once more goes downhill and flows through the valleys. Moreover, a valley may remain in the shade for hours after the sun has touched the mountaintops. The coldest time in a mountain valley may be a few hours after the sun rises.

Wind patterns in the mountains can be complex. Mountains, obviously, can block the wind. On the other hand, the wind hitting mountains is often forced to move along them and find some release point. Thus, a wind may hit a mountain wall and move along it until it comes to a pass and go shooting through it. Some mountain passes are extremely windy at times. The wind patterns can only be studied while in the mountains as they vary so.

In trying to determine whether or not a day is windy in the mountains you can have problems. Sometimes the wind will be blowing very hard and the sky can be clear and cloudless. However, there are times when you can see wind clouds over the mountains. You can recognize them as they have two characteristics. One, they hover

A mirage seen on the Matterhorn. Atmospheric conditions at high altitudes occasionally produce unusual phenomena. (*Courtesy Swiss National Tourist Office*)

over the mountains. Second, they are flat and streamlined looking. Frequently, they are dark and sort of dirty looking.

Another wind cloud is in the shape of ripples or waves which lie parallel to the mountains. They too indicate high winds. Of course, in the winter when there is loose snow on the peaks, you can easily see blowing snow or snow plumes.

Occasionally you encounter strange optical effects in the mountains. Some are extremely impressive. One of the great sights on earth is to stand on Pikes Peak at sunset. From the summit you can see some 150 miles. Just at sunset, you can see the huge black shadow of the peak suddenly sweep forward, moving at a great rate of speed toward the eastern horizon. This, of course, would be true of any such isolated peak surrounded either to the west or east by flatlands. Of course, the morning shadow races backward toward the peak.

It sometimes happens that climbers will be standing on a peak and near them will be clouds, upon which their shadows will be magnified. Pretty strange.

Another strange effect produced by clouds is that distant city lights will sometimes be seen through low-lying clouds. The clouds diffuse the lights and at the same time seem to lift them. When that happens the city lights will look like a galaxy of stars.

Sometimes the sun, as seen through blowing ice crystals, will appear as though it were in the center of a luminous cross. Such effects startled early climbers in the Alps, for they took them as mysterious signs.

Ice crystals also form sun dogs. You might look up in the sky when there is a veil of clouds overhead and suddenly see in the sky another sun. In fact, for a moment you might be quite unsure of which is which.

I mention all of these things to point out some of the rewards of mountain climbing and the strange beauty which you can encounter in the mountains far and away above the rest of the world.

16

High-altitude Effects and Problems

As we all know, the earth is surrounded by a blanket of air. It is dense at sea level, most dense in deep mines and places below sea level, and less dense at higher elevations. The air does not change much in its composition at different altitudes. About 20 percent of the atmosphere at sea level is oxygen; and at the top of Mount Everest, the world's highest peak, which rises 29,002 feet, the air still has about 20 per cent oxygen. However, there is considerably less oxygen simply because there is less air.

A high-altitude camp in the Chugach Mountains of Alaska. Notice the pyramidical-shaped tent. (*Courtesy the American Alpine Club*)

It is convenient for a climber to remember that at 18,000 feet above sea level there is one half as much air as there is at sea level. At 36,000 feet, roughly, there is only one fourth as much air. Knowing that, you can make a chart of the amount of air at any elevation. The accompanying chart is somewhat more accurate, because the density of the air does not decrease at a perfectly uniform rate as the altitude increases. No chart is completely accurate, though, as the air pressure varies in the mountains just as it does at sea level.

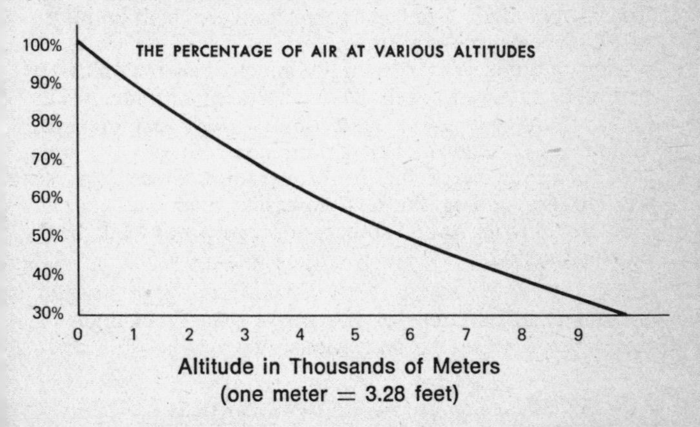

From the chart you can determine, for instance, that at the top of Mount Whitney, which is the highest mountain in the forty-eight mainland states, 14,495 feet (approximately 4,420 meters) above sea level, there would be only about 60 per cent as much air as at sea level. Most people suffer from the effects of altitude at such a height. I once saw a very strong college athlete pass out cold on top of Pikes Peak, whereas a somewhat overweight middle-aged man who climbed with him did not seem bothered. However, the athlete "rushed" the mountain and the middle-aged man slowly walked up it, which could explain everything.

The higher the altitude, the more difficult it is to become acclimatized, for it takes longer for the body to adjust. As with most things, people adjust at different rates. There is, however, a point where the body simply cannot make adjustments any longer. For many years it was thought that one could adjust to very high altitudes, such as 26,000 feet above sea level. Tests have shown that this is not the case. At altitudes of more than about 22,000 feet above sea level the body cannot adjust, even though the person may feel okay. At that altitude and above, there is always a lack of oxygen in the cells. In fact, they begin to die. The longer one remains above such altitudes the more cells die. Some cells can replace themselves, but brain cells cannot. This helps explain why there is no city on earth more than 18,000 feet above sea level. People of all races wisely stayed below the danger zones. Today mountain climbers going to very high altitudes often carry oxygen with them.

High altitude does not simply affect one's breathing. It has other effects as well. With increased altitude, water boils at an ever lower temperature. Early explorers in mountainous regions often determined altitudes by boiling water and recording its temperature. Since it is so easy to do, and is far less expensive than carrying an altimeter, though more bother, you can always fall back on this method.

THE TEMPERATURES OF BOILING WATER AT VARIOUS ALTITUDES

Altitude	Temperature
Sea level	100° C or 212° F
5,000 ft.	95° C or 203° F
10,000 ft.	90° C or 194° F
15,000 ft.	85° C or 185° F

The temperature of boiling water drops one degree Fahrenheit for every 555 feet gained in elevation, and one degree Celsius for every 1,000 feet. As mentioned earlier, the cooler temperatures of boiling water at high altitudes interferes with cooking.

At high altitudes, your skin and lips dry out faster. It is always wise to put a cream which screens the sun on exposed parts of the body. Some are made especially for blocking the harmful ultraviolet rays. Prevention is far easier than the cure. Lips should also be protected. Many corner-drugstore sticks are not too good. It is better to get a lip cream which is sold by stores specializing in mountaineering equipment. Also be sure to protect your nose.

The frequently dry air increases your thirst. Most

people's sinuses dry out rapidly in the air. For the first few days, this can be a minor annoyance.

Many climbers at high altitudes have complained about a loss of appetite, as mentioned before. This can be serious, as you need food for fuel when you are doing hard work. If you do not eat enough, you will get progressively weaker. I was once told a story about a man who owned a mine located about 12,000 feet above sea level. Every morning he checked to see how much the miners ate for breakfast so he could determine how much work they would do that day.

One difficulty is that of breathing. At higher altitudes it becomes ever harder to breathe. At 18,000 feet above sea level you must take many more breaths per minute than at sea level to make up for the fact that there is less air. You would think that you should take twice as many breaths to get as much air. It never works out quite like that, as there are too many things to consider: blood cell count, fatigue, the fact that it is more difficult to "suck" thinner air into the lungs, since there is not as much pressure outside pushing it in. The fact is, however, that you automatically breathe harder, but not twice as hard, because the heart is beating more rapidly at high altitudes.

At high altitudes, you often have trouble thinking clearly. This is partly due to exhaustion, but also due to a lack of oxygen. One of the most common complaints is that you begin to believe you are with the wrong number of people. Thus, someone climbing a mountain with two others may begin to think there is a fourth person. Edmund Hillary, who first climbed Mount Everest, thought someone else had climbed it. It took him a while to realize he himself had just climbed it. Simple tasks become quite confusing, such as doing camera work. Many people have made the wrong settings on their cameras when getting ready for the "summit shot."

Mental confusion can also be a symptom and warning that you are getting too chilled and your bodily processes are slowing down. It is difficult to tell how much is due to one cause or another, and when you become aware of such symptoms, your state must be *closely watched.*

One effect of the high altitude is that you often begin to lack will power. At just the point you seem to need it the most, it is not available.

Some people have tried to overcome the effects of high altitude. There are some climbers who have smoked cigarettes. The idea has been that inhaling the smoke made them more aware that they were actually breathing. I do not recommend it. A few, encouraged by pictures of nice big St. Bernard dogs leaping across the snows of the Alps carrying brandy to people, have felt that a good stiff drink would help. The truth is that alcohol slows down the amount of oxygen going to the brain, thus it can only worsen the situation.

At high altitudes you can fall asleep much too easily. I have seen climbers just sit down in the snow and snooze. That is okay, but I read of a famous climber who fell sound asleep while on belay, which is a method of protecting a rock climber on a rope.

17

Rock Climbing

It is important for a rock climber to know as much about the nature of cliffs as possible. First, many mountains are shaped in such a way that they have steep cliffs on all sides. These are called faces, and are named according to the side of the mountain on which they are located. Naming faces this way is handy, for a climber immediately knows something about it. For example, in the Northern Hemisphere the north faces of mountains do not receive any direct sunlight—ever. Thus, north faces are colder. Also, glaciers are usually bigger and more active on them, and since glaciers are what make steep cliffs, the north face of a mountain will be the steepest of all. By the same token, an east face will have sunlight on it in the morning and a west face in the afternoon, whereas a south face will be the sunniest and warmest of all.

Walls are steep cliffs. Those found in Yosemite Valley, for example, really look like walls, being almost perpendicular. Furthermore they are quite smooth, for the most part lack cracks and ledges. Cliffs steeper than sixty degrees—anywhere up to ninety degrees, perpendicular—are considered walls. Sixty degrees may not sound like much. However, if you are actually on such a cliff it seems extremely steep. A climber would call anything from thirty to sixty degrees a steep slope, and anything up to thirty degrees a gentle slope.

There are terms which refer to the size of cracks found in cliffs. Rock climbers use the term cracks for anything small enough to place a piton in. Fortunately most cliffs have plenty of them. A fissure is a crack which is too

Two rock climbers working their way up a cliff in Switzerland. Such climbing often allows you to see dramatic and interesting scenery. (*Courtesy Swiss National Tourist Office*)

wide for a piton, but not large enough for you to squeeze your body into. Many, however, are large enough for you to put in a leg or an arm. A chimney is a crack large enough for a climber to get inside of. It has to be such that a climber can brace himself within it. Chimneys are an important natural feature found on a reasonable number of cliffs. Lastly a gully is a crack large enough to walk around inside of. Couloir (a French term, pronounced "coo-lwar") is another name for a gully.

Quite often two cliffs will meet the way two walls of a room meet in a corner. Some climbers call it an open-book formation, as it resembles the gutter of a book where two pages meet. It is also called a diedre (pronounced "dee-aidr"), the French word for dihedral, which is the angle formed by two planes meeting. An open-book formation usually offers a climber a route upward, because in most cases there is a good crack in the cliff where the two walls meet.

The term ridge hardly needs to be explained. A sharp ridge is called an arete ("uh-rate"). A rib is an outward portion of a cliff which is more or less vertical. It resembles a pilaster, which is a column attached to the side of a building. A spur is a projecting ridge, resembling the smaller veins of a leaf coming outward from the mid-vein.

A pinnacle is a free-standing rock which can be a thousand feet or more in height or only thirty feet. Gendarmes are pinnacles or piles of rock found on ridges. Aiguille ("a-gweel") is the French name for a particularly sharp pinnacle. Towers are self-explanatory. Climbers sometimes call big, fat pinnacles towers, and the term can also refer to huge peaks such as the Muztagh Tower —a giant peak in Asia over 20,000 feet high.

Ledges are more or less horizontal shelves, which can vary in width from almost nothing to something broader than a sidewalk.

Cliffs and slopes can be made up of a wide variety of rock. Moreover, the rock found at one part of a cliff can vary greatly from that found at a higher elevation or on another part of the cliff. Some rock is much harder and tougher than other rock. For example, granite is tough but chalk can break easily. A climber needs to check out the toughness of rock before trusting it, as some rocks will not hold a piton well. Loose rock that breaks easily is rotten in all senses of the word. Rocks weather differently. Sandstone, for example, often weathers in such a way that numerous holes and pockets form on it which make good handholds.

Often the way a rock splits determines what type of handhold it will give. Many rocks are laid down in strata. From a distance they can sometimes look like large pieces of cardboard laid one on top of another. The strata or layers are not always level. The tilt of the various layers can influence greatly the type of handholds you will have. On tilted layers, the upper parts of the layers offer better handholds, as the angles of the rock are better. Such layers often go right through a mountain and one side of the mountain is easier to climb than another side, even sometimes if it is steeper. The famous Matterhorn was climbed on a steep side first because the layers of rock on that side offered better handholds than on a less-steep side. In looking over a cliff, try to find out as much as you can about the nature of its rock.

Many cliffs have dirt, rubble, broken stone, or gravel on them. Dirt is loose and therefore not to be trusted. A good handhold covered with dirt, even if it is packed

Layers of rock going through a mountain. Notice that it would be much easier to climb the right-hand side of the mountain though it is much steeper than the left side. The reason is apparent in the shape of the handholds. Those on the right-hand side would be far easier to use.

down, can be almost worthless. Gravel is maybe even worse. Some ledges covered with gravel are like stairs covered with ball bearings. In general, cliffs covered with loose materials are dangerous. Any vegetation is a nuisance; remember that a tree never makes a good support. It is next to impossible to know how strong a tree is. Some are decayed, some have weak roots, and so on. Never use a tree or bush while climbing. Grassy slopes, as we have mentioned, are dangerous. More than one climber has arrived at the top of a cliff and started to walk across grass, only to fall. In checking a cliff, see if it is topped by grass or loose materials of any kind.

In choosing a cliff be sure that you and your companions understand the nature of the cliff. You should, of course, choose one that you know can be easily managed by *you*. The importance of this cannot be overstressed.

If most of the cliff does not seem difficult for you, then choose a route up it. First look for dangerous areas. Rocks falling down a cliff are the most usual danger. Look at the base of cliffs and see if there are rocks there. Stay away from such areas. Stay away from ice and snow. Carefully study the cliff and plan a route which includes wide ledges, places where there are plenty of cracks for pitons, good resting places, or chimneys and ridges you can cross. Most routes call for both some vertical climbing and traverses, which are more or less horizontal routes. Thus, one may climb up a chimney, traverse the cliff along a ledge, and finally climb up a ridge. Plan.

Look at the cliff you wish to climb and know exactly where you will be going. Do not make the mistake of going two thirds of the way up and then finding out you do not know how to proceed. At times that could be a dangerous mistake to make. The more consideration put into route planning the better and safer the climb will be.

When you begin a rock climb you and your companion or companions will need to rope up. It is sometimes best for a beginner to be placed in the middle of the rope between two experts. This affords him a great deal more safety.

Before roping up, check the ropes and see that they

are in perfect condition. There are several ways to tie on to a climbing rope, but the best way for a beginner is as follows. Take a ¼-inch-diameter hemp rope and put it around your body seven times, loosely. Tie it together with a fisherman's knot. Be absolutely positive the knot is correct and have a more experienced climber check it for you.

The fisherman's knot. (*Photograph by Alexander Smith*)

The fisherman's knot tightened. Notice how it should fit together smoothly. (*Photograph by Alexander Smith*)

Attach to the seven loops of rope a carabiner which has a screw that closes the gate tightly and securely. Put it on so that when you hold out the carabiner the screw is on the underside. Since all seven strands of rope are in it, you are secured to the carabiner by the strength of seven ropes. Tie the main climbing rope on to the carabiner with an overhand figure-eight knot. This knot

Figure-eight knot in a loop. (*Photograph by the author*)

can easily be made at the end or at the middle of the rope. Check the pictures of the knots in this book and, once more, have the most experienced climber in the group check it for you. If you have tied on to the end, you should have at least about eight inches of the loose end of the rope hanging beyond the knot, but be sure it does not hang down too far.

The correct way to attach a rope. The rock climber has a seven-rope waist band on. To it is attached a screw-type carabiner. The climbing rope, in turn, is attached to that by a figure-eight knot in a loop. Note: In actual practice the screw on the carabiner must be tightened so it will not open. Furthermore, the carabiner must be rotated so that the screw attachment is facing downward. (*Photograph by the author*)

Men often like to have the manila around the waist. On the other hand, some climbers, including myself, like to have it up under the armpits, secured there by a rope over one shoulder. Women should have the ropes high and above the breasts. The reason for having the rope high is that if you do fall, you will not tip over backward and land upside down, which, to say the least, can make things difficult.

Later a beginner can use a harness, which is in some ways easier to use. However, for safety's safe, all beginners should know how to tie on with just ropes. There is a simpler way yet, which I do not recommend for beginners. You can tie on to the climbing rope itself with a bowline knot and not use a carabiner. For years this was the standard way of doing things. But some people have trouble tying the knot correctly and the single rope puts a great deal of pressure on you if you fall. The seven-rope method puts less pressure on you, and the harness the least amount.

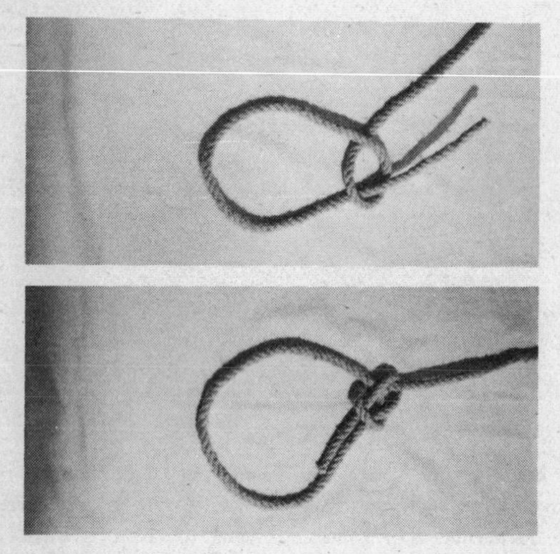

Bowline knot. The first photograph shows how to start it; the second shows the completed bowline. (*Photograph by the author*)

You are all roped up. Now what? The lead person is the most experienced climber in the group. He or she goes first and starts forward and, if it is possible, free climbs, meaning he climbs without any aids at all. Of course, a beginner would not be on a climb which required direct aids. The beginner would be right behind the leader. Before the leader starts off, the beginner will have taken the rope and coiled it. As the leader moves forward, the beginner will slowly let out loop after loop of rope, always being sure that it is neat and that there is a slight bit of tension on it so that it does not sag down over rocks where it might catch on anything. The leader moves until he is either at the end of the rope or at a good place to stop.

The leader may have to belay the beginner. We will see later how that is done. If the leader is on belay, he will holler down to the beginner, "On belay!" This means that the leader is ready to help the beginner up. No one should ever move until he hears that call. If the leader is on belay, he will pull the rope so that there is no slack.

One of the most difficult places to climb is from the base of a cliff to a point about thirty feet up it. It gives the leader almost no chance to protect the beginner. Thus, in choosing a cliff, watch out for the first thirty feet.

Climbers never touch the rope. Some people have the mistaken idea that a leader goes up and the next goes hand over hand. Well, it is not like that at all. The beginner climbs up the rocks using his hands and feet.

If you begin to fall, you yell, "Falling!" This warning gives the leader a split-second opportunity to get into action and hold you.

Everything mentioned so far should be practiced. Beginners should go to a rock climbing school where they will have the opportunity to fall and be held. As you fall on a rope, there are ways of safeguarding yourself. First, the head must be protected. An attempt should be made to stay out away from the cliff, as well as an attempt not to fall upside down. Practice helps a great deal in getting the feel of a fall.

Once the beginner is next to the leader and the leader stops belaying him, he says, "Off belay." The ropes must once more be put in order. The beginner will again coil them neatly and let them out when the leader once more moves forward. The process is repeated as many times as needed.

If the beginner is in the middle of a rope between two experts, he must see to it that the rope is taken in when the third person is coming up. It will be the beginner's responsibility to coil it in his hands and keep the rope between his hands and the third person without slack.

Two climbers are making their way up a steep cliff. The lead climber is belaying the other one. (*Courtesy the American Alpine Club*)

When you rock-climb, move as gracefully as possible. Always stand out from the cliff so that your weight goes down *straight* into your boots. In this way you get more traction with your feet. If you lean in toward the cliff, you lose traction and your feet are not gripping the cliff securely enough. This often takes practice, as most people tend to lean toward a cliff. Be positive in your motions, but loose. Balance is obviously important, and if a person has a poor sense of balance, he probably should not go rock climbing. The biggest muscles are in your legs and they are far stronger than your arms. Thus rock climb-

Many inexperienced climbers stand incorrectly on a steep slope. The man on the left is leaning in, which is wrong. The man on the right is standing up straight, which is correct, for his weight goes straight down into his boots and so his feet grip the mountain better. You should always stand upright on such slopes.

ing is not a matter of pulling yourself up with your hands and arms. Good rock climbing is done with the legs, and the arms and hands are used as little as possible.

Never use your knees to lift yourself up. The knee joint is one of the weakest of all and it can easily be thrown out of whack. Always look at least three steps ahead, knowing beforehand exactly where you are going to move to and how you are going to do it. Sometimes you have to plan exactly where you will put your hands and feet before doing so. It is, of course, best to watch the leader and see how he crosses difficult spots. Never get spread-eagled—that is, into a position where you have your two arms out at full length and your legs at full length. Obviously, if you got into such a position, you could not move forward. You keep on a cliff by three points, either two hands and one foot, or two feet and one hand. You use the fourth limb to move forward with.

In climbing, do not, if at all possible, climb above someone else. If you do, you might dislodge a rock and it will fall on the person. Worse, if someone falls on another, the two people may both fall.

It is important to know about various handholds. First, the steepness of a cliff often has little to do with the quality or quantity of good handholds. I remember once in the Garden of the Gods, Colorado, worrying about a very steep cliff ahead of me while I was on one much less steep. Actually, the very steep cliff was far easier, for it had good handholds.

Ledges provide handholds. The best ledges have a shape

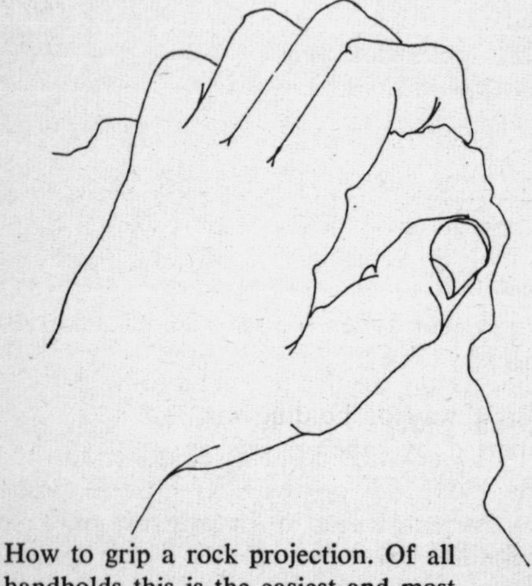

How to grip a rock projection. Of all handholds this is the easiest and most secure.

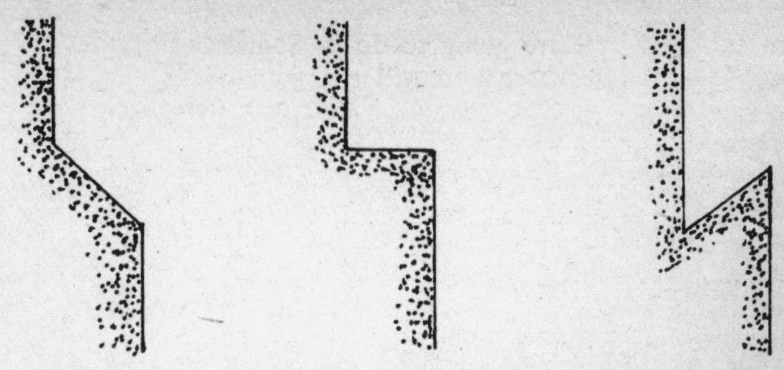

Profiles of various possible handholds. The one on the left slopes and therefore can only be used as a pressure hold from above. You can push downward into it, especially with the palm of the hand. The next one is good and can be used to grip from below. The third is a "jug handle" and is easily gripped from below. Both the second and third can also be used as footholds.

like an upside-down V. You can easily grasp them. Some climbers call them jug handles. Not only do they offer good handholds, but once you are further up the cliff, they double as footholds. The next best ledges are at right angles like a window sill. They too give good handholds but not quite as good as those you can grasp. The worst ledges are those that slant downward so that you never quite get a good grasp. If such handholds are above you, they will not afford good support, though they sometimes can be used. If one is below your chest, you can use it better by putting the heel of your hand on it and pushing. If the slant is not too great, the pressure of your weight into the heel of your hand will hold you.

Many ledges are wide enough that you can place your fingers over them and obtain a grip. If a ledge is very narrow, you can often place your fingers in such a position that they are tightly curled together. You place the tips of the fingers on the ledge and thus grip it. This is not the securest way of holding on, but it will work if you are supported by other points as well. Of course, some ledges are too narrow even for that grip.

Quite often you will encounter a horizontal crack which slants upward into the cliff. You can grasp the underside of the upper part, very much as you would grasp a wooden drawer handle which you take palm up-

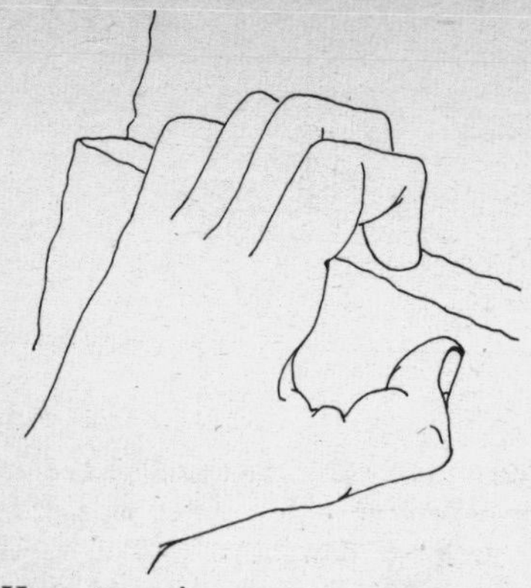

How to grip a very narrow handhold.

wards. You cannot, of course, use such a handhold if it is above you, but if it is somewhat lower than your elbow, you can. At times it gives you a very secure grip.

Another not-so-obvious handhold involves the use of a deep horizontal or vertical crack. You thrust your hand into it, make a fist, and turn the fist to lock into it. You cannot put too much weight on an arm in that position, but it can help in moving from one place to another. If a crack is larger and it is feasible, you can sometimes jam your elbow into the crack and pull your fist back toward your shoulder, which will make the

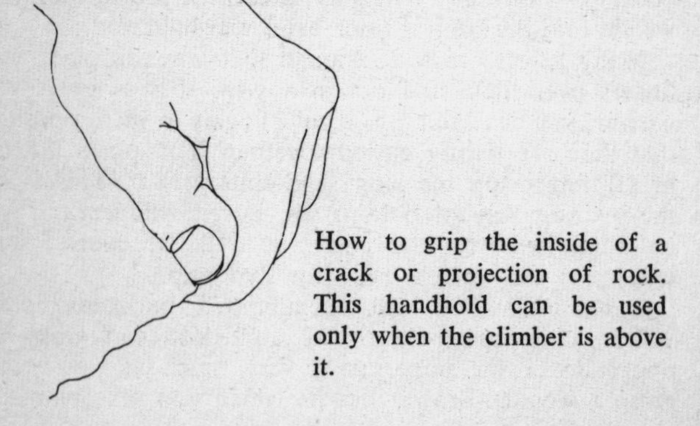

How to grip the inside of a crack or projection of rock. This handhold can be used only when the climber is above it.

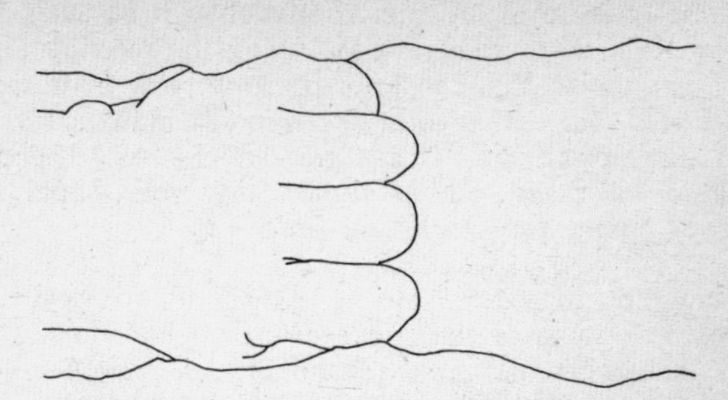

The fist jam. You can place your hand into a narrow crack, then make a fist of it. The fist swells up and grips the sides of the crack.

elbow bulge outward, tightening it in the crack. Because this is both a difficult grip to use and lessens your forward motion, it is not used much. Anyway, it is not particularly strong.

In some narrower cracks you can put your fingers in the rock and then arch the fingers upward. This will hold only if you are already supported. It is more for balance.

Another finger grip is used when you must move forward in front of a vertical crack. You can put the fingers of both hands in it and pull sideways against them. This is not a secure hold either, but can help in moving from one point to another if you are supported by your legs.

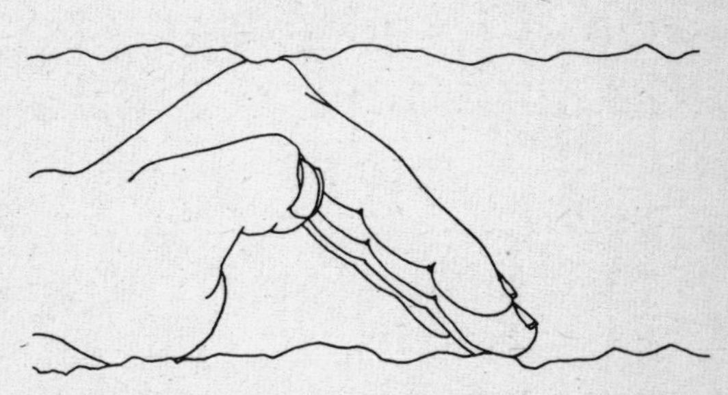

The finger jam hold. You can place your hand into a crack and then arch the palm of the hand and fingers. This provides a hold.

Quite often an open-book formation will be such that two walls meet at right angles. Along the meeting place there is a crack. You can grip the crack with both hands and place your feet against the opposite wall and work your way up the cliff. This works, and a strong beginner could do it easily, but as it is tiring, you should not plan on going very high that way.

Footholds, in general, are not as difficult for beginners to learn as some of the above described handholds. Not only that, what has been a handhold one minute often becomes a foothold the next, so the separation between them is at times artificial.

Ledges, obviously, are a major type of foothold. Large ledges on which you can fully stand are, of course, the

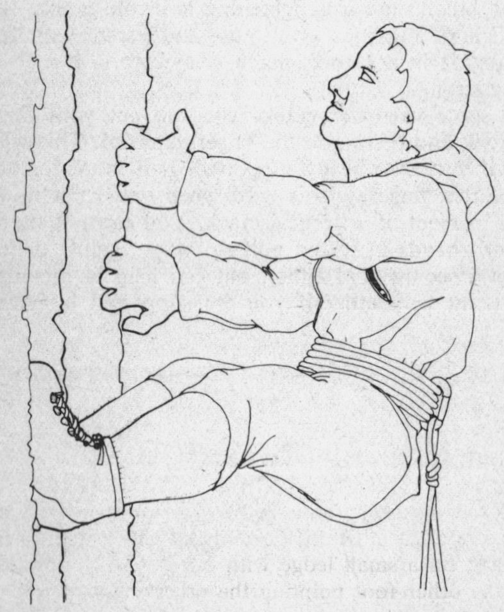

The layback. You have your hands in a crack and your feet against a wall. By pushing your feet against the wall and holding on with your hands, you can make your way upward along the crack.

A climber in a chimney. You can easily jam yourself in a chimney by placing your back against one side of it and pushing against the other side with your feet. Once in such a position, it is not at all difficult to work your way upward.

best. Many ledges, however, are narrow, and you cannot get a whole foot on them.

In general, it is best to toe into the cliff, with the toes on the ledge. When you do, keep the heel down below the level of your toes. Get as much of your foot onto the ledge as possible. Once you feel that you have planted your foot firmly, do not move it. Do not move your heel, especially in an upward motion.

Sometimes you get a better foothold when you stand on a narrow ledge with either the inside or the outside of the boot in close to the cliff. At times it may be best to stand on a small ledge with one foot pointing outward and the other foot pointing the other way.

From the above descriptions it becomes obvious why rock climbing boots have such narrow welts. The narrower they are, the more you can get your foot into the cliff.

Quite a few vertical cracks become narrower as they

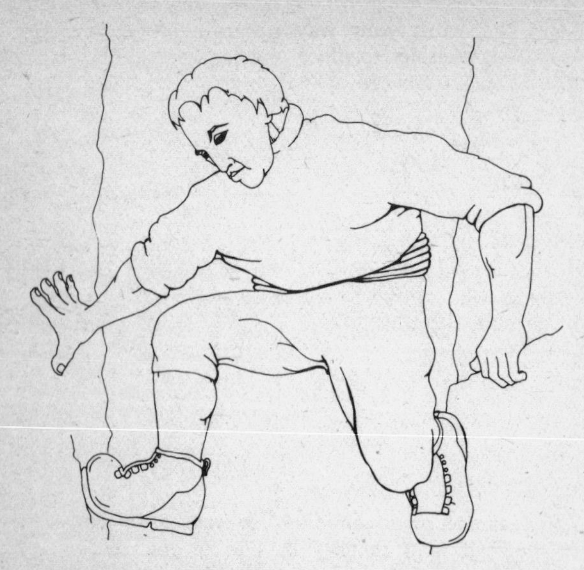

A climber working his way up a chimney. He is pressing against the sides of the chimney with his hands and feet.

go down a cliff. If so, you can place a boot into the crack and jam it. You have to have heavy boots on to do so, or at least ones whose soles will not bend upward at the edges. Be very careful of this one, as you can get the boot caught. It is usually best to put the boot in at an angle; then in taking it out, straighten it and pull it back.

Most beginners like to climb in chimneys. They give you a sense of security once you get the hang of it. They are quite easy to manage, and when you are climbing in one, you know that you are engaged in real mountain climbing.

Choose one which is free of any signs of falling rocks. It should be just wide enough so that you can get your back up against one side and place your feet against the other side in such a way that your knees are bent, not too much and not too little. Once you are in a chimney in that position, you should be able with no trouble to push against it and hold yourself inside of it. Once secure in it, you can work your way up in a sort of sitting position, but it is easier to place one leg back under your buttocks and push upward with it, along with your other leg and arms.

If the chimney has rough sides, and most do, you can easily straddle it, having one foot and one hand on one side and one on the other. In actual practice, you find all of this surprisingly easy to do.

Every now and then you will be forced to cross a horizontal knife-edged ridge. The easiest and safest way of crossing one is to sit on it horseback style. As you straddle it, you can easily move yourself along with your hands by pushing down on the ridge and inching forward.

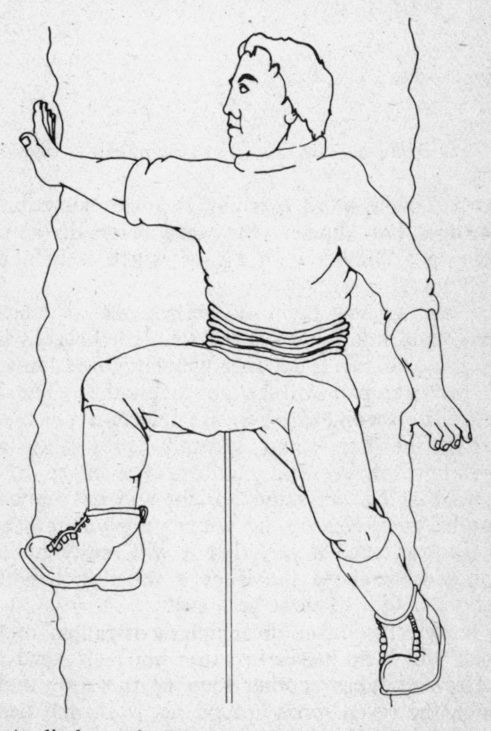

A climber using another position as he climbs up a chimney, pushing against the sides of it with his hands and feet.

A very steep, narrow ridge can be climbed as shown.

Belay is an old word meaning to make something fast with a rope. For climbers the word refers to a method for securing a climber with a rope which is held by another climber.

There are several types of belays, all of which the climber should know. One is the shoulder belay, which is accomplished in the following manner. One climber, the leader, for example, will be above another. The leader will belay the second climber. He selects a place on the cliff where he can stand securely, preferably almost directly above the second climber. The place must be chosen so that he can stand upright and have good support for his feet. Nearby, he pounds a piton into a horizontal crack in such a way that it will really hold. This piton should be above the leader's waist in height, and from about a foot to three feet away.

The leader then takes the climbing rope and makes a loop in it which he places in a carabiner attached to the piton. He next takes another loop of the rope and puts it through the seven ropes around his waist and ties it to them with a two-half-hitch knot. Thus he is secured to the piton by two sections of the main climbing rope. If he is ever pulled against them, he will be held by two strands of the climbing rope. He is secured to the cliff, and it would be very difficult for him to be pulled off.

Once the leader is sure that he is properly secured to the cliff, he can start the belay proper. He grasps the climbing rope with his right hand, if he is right-handed, in such a way that that rope to the climber below has no slack. The rope goes from the leader's right hand over his back and left shoulder. With the left arm crooked, he grasps the rope with the left hand. From the left hand, the remaining rope continues on to the knot in the seven-rope loop.

If the climber below falls, the leader can hold him or her without fear of being pulled off the cliff. The leader must be very careful to see that any extra rope is coiled

The two-half-hitch. The knot is made with the loop of rope, which goes around the seven-rope waist band. The rope to the climber's back goes to a piton. The rope to the front goes to the other climber. The end of the rope is hanging over it. The knot will hold the climber on to the piton. The purpose of the knot is so that the climber is secured to the piton by a double rope. (*Photograph by the author*)

The shoulder belay. The climber on the left is belaying the one on the right. Notice how the ropes of the belayer go into the piton behind him. The knot is a two-half-hitch made with the loop.

in such a way that if the climber below falls and the rope moves through the leader's hands, as it will and is supposed to do, it will not catch the leader's feet, suddenly snag a rock below, or get tangled in any way.

When the leader feels he is ready and that everything is all right, he calls down to the other climber, "On belay!" This, as we've seen, is a signal that it is safe for him to begin climbing toward the leader. As the second climber starts to move upward, he calls, "Climbing." The leader keeps the rope fairly taut, but not so tight that it interferes with the climber's motions. The reason for having it taut is to arrest a fall as quickly as possible. If a person falls he quickly gathers speed. Obviously, the faster the fall the harder it will be to stop. A split second can matter.

If the second climber falls, he should immediately call up, "Falling," so that the leader has a second chance to tighten the rope. It is almost impossible to stop a person with a jolt. It is easier to let some rope slide down with the falling person and bring the person to a slow stop. The farther the person actually free-falls, the less chance the leader has of bringing him to any sort of quick stop, thus more rope must be let out. The rope which is let out slides through the leader's hand and over his shoulder. Since this can cause a rope burn, climbers should wear leather gloves and have some padding on the shoulder from a jacket. Even if the leader cannot completely stop the fall of the other climber with his hands, he can at least slow it down considerably so that when the rope gets to the knot in the leader's seven-rope coil it will stop without the rope breaking.

The call "Off belay" is used by the belayer when he is finished to warn the climber not to climb. The call "Rock" means a rock is falling—beware! The climber calls, "Slack," for more rope. He calls, "Rope," to pull excess rope. He calls, "Tension," when he wants the belayer to pull like crazy and hold him.

It is best to mention that there are some alternate ways of attaching the rope to the piton. The main climbing rope can go from the carabiner attached to the leader's seven-rope coil to and through a carabiner in the piton and back to the climber. Instead of attaching it with a two-half-hitch knot, the leader can take the climbing rope and tie in it with a figure-eight knot, exactly like those used for tying on to the rope. He can attach that loop to another carabiner, also hooked on to the seven-

A climber belaying a leader with a sitting belay. If the lead man falls, the belayer can "sit" back against the rope. Thus his own weight can help to stop the fall. In practicing this belay, you should see what sort of grip is best for your left hand. Some prefer it as shown. Use the strongest and most comfortable grip you can. Note how the belayer's ropes are attached to the piton.

rope coil. In this arrangement he is once more secured to the piton by two strands of rope. In some ways it is a better and easier arrangement.

Of course, people who are left-handed should reverse the shoulder belay. The rope from the other climber comes up to the leader's left hand and over the right shoulder to the right hand.

In most climbs a second climber must belay the leader. The second climber cannot use the shoulder belay, as he or she will be belaying someone above. Belay the leader in a different fashion. First you secure yourself in a place where you can stand. Next, place a piton in a horizontal crack and secure yourself to it exactly the way the leader did during a shoulder belay, except that the piton is best placed about waist level. Above the climber and a couple feet or so to the right or left, place another secure piton.

The rope from the leader, who is above the second piton, goes through a carabiner attached to the second piton. It then goes through the right hand of the climber, around, and slightly below, the buttocks and to the left hand.

If the leader falls, he will fall in such a way that he will be below the second piton. The pull on the rope for the belaying climber will be toward the second piton. The climber can hold the leader by letting some rope out and bringing him to an even stop without a jolt. Moreover, because the rope is under the buttocks, he can exert pressure on it by "sitting" on it, adding his whole weight to the pull.

On a difficult climb the leader will place several pitons between himself and the belaying one; such an arrangement is called a running belay. Warning: A leader falling from ten feet above the piton falls twenty feet. A leader can rarely be saved if he falls that far.

The sitting belay just described can also be used by a leader who is above another climber. To use it, place a second piton above yourself, higher than your shoulders. Then you can place the rope from yourself to the other climber through its carabiner.

Most climbers use a sitting hip belay when possible. The rope passes behind the belayer's back, usually at the level of his hips, below the seven-rope coil. In the sitting hip belay the belayer sits and braces his legs in the direction of the climber. Thus, he can push against any tension if the climber falls. It is often difficult to find a place to set up such a belay. If you can, use it, for it is the safest and best belay.

All belayers must be sure always to brace against a fall. The leg on the side where the pull will come is straight and locked. If a fall comes, the body must be so that it will not twist. Also be certain any fall will pull you toward the cliff and not away from it. Never take your hands off the ropes. To move them, slide them. Always keep a grip on the guide hand.

It cannot be stressed too much that all of these belays must be learned from an experienced climber and practiced before ever being used. You cannot learn them when someone is actually falling and the belay is needed. At that time, you must have already learned what to do.

In placing pitons and carabiners, it is important to see that the rope can always slide freely through them. The leader should not have to tug at the rope to get it through the carabiners. It can upset his balance. A carabiner in a piton is placed gate upward so a downward push against a rock does not open it.

Sometimes it is very difficult to place pitons in such a way that the rope will not be dragged along rock edges. However, you can take a nylon rope the same diameter as the climbing rope and make slings. The sling is a loop of rope tied securely to itself with fisherman's knots. In this instance, a climber places the rope sling through the eye of the piton. To that is attached a carabiner. If the sling is long enough, the climbing rope going through the carabiner on the loop will not scrape against the edges of the rocks.

Direct climbing is not something a beginner would normally concern himself with. It is a method used for going up cliffs devoid of handholds but which have vertical cracks. You might use it for short cliffs. It is actually quite simple. The method involves the use of small ladders, also called étriers (pronounced "a-tree-ays"). They are often made of webbed nylon. Use two of them. Pound in pitons in the vertical crack and attach the ladders, which you climb, one after the other, as many times as needed. You must of course be sure you have a good belay.

Many climbers frown on this type of climbing. They feel it really is not mountain climbing at all, saying it is really more the sort of thing you might do if you were going to climb a building to repair something.

There is, however, one technique which is more disliked by mountain climbers. You might wonder what would happen if you came to an absolutely sheer wall without handholds, footholds, or cracks. Unfortunately, some climbers take along rock drills. There are some, called star drills, which can be held in the hands. The climbers put on safety goggles and drill a hole as high as they can. Into the hole they place expansion bolts and onto them they place small ladders. Such holes mar a cliff. They destroy the natural beauty of the rock. Do not use this method. Discourage it.

You might wonder how climbers can climb a cliff where the rocks protrude outward. First, most of the time you can go around an overhang. A large overhang, however, is overcome by the use of small rope ladders and pitons, very much like vertical cracks are used. The technique is to place the pitons in the roof of the overhang, place a nylon web ladder on it, stand on the ladder over "nothing," and place another piton farther along the overhang. Then place another ladder there, move to it, release the first ladder, and continue. Of course, you would be belayed to the pitons on the roof. In many respects, overhangs are not as difficult as you might think, but they require an experienced climber.

The word rappelling refers to a method whereby a climber can get down from a steep cliff using a rope. As you know, there are many places where you can climb up, but not down. This is extremely important to remember, as no one should ever go up a cliff, get in some difficult place, and not be able to go up or down.

Climbers descend difficult areas by rappelling down over the rocks. There are several ways in which it is done. All climbers should, first of all, know how to do it without any special equipment. You might have to get down from a cliff with just a climbing rope.

Most rappel ropes are secured to a piton. In this case, the rope does go through the eye of the piton. The rope is fastened there at its midpoint. In starting the rappel, face toward the piton. At that moment your back is toward the cliff. Put the rope between your legs, bring it back over the left buttock, in front, over, and across the chest and over the right shoulder. The right hand guides the rope and the left hand can either grip it, pull it back across the body, or do both at the same time. Then back down over the cliff. It is difficult for most people to walk backward over a cliff fifty or a hundred feet high, but it can be done easily after a few tries.

The proper form is for the climber to rappel so that he is perpendicular to the face of the cliff. Thus, if the cliff is ninety degrees, you will be parallel with the ground below. Both legs should be slightly apart and your boot soles full against the cliff. Some people like to release the rope a bit and float downward in great leaps, but such a practice is not really safe. It is better to more or less

A rappeller "walking" along the cliff. You can often use a rappelling technique as a means to explore the face of a cliff, as this climber is doing.

walk down the cliff in a series of hops. This puts much less strain on the rope. Have a knot in the lower part of the rope so that you know when you are near the end of it.

All members of a climbing party shoud be belayed while they are rappelling, particularly beginners. There have been accidents while people were rappelling. Occasionally while climbing it is next to impossible for the last person down to be belayed and he must go down as safely as possible. It is always possible to get rope burns in rappelling, so wear a heavy jacket and leather gloves.

Rappelling is an absolute must to learn. The easiest places to learn are on slopes of about forty-five degrees, such as you might find on a road cut. After learning on an intermediate slope, try steeper ones until you have mastered a perpendicular one. It is good to try rappelling from an overhang and go down through the air without touching the cliff.

You can use a lighter rope for rappelling than for climbing, and some climbers carry them. A ¼-inch nylon rope capable of holding 1,000 pounds is often used. It is doubled, so that it can hold almost 2,000 pounds. The usual length is 500 feet so that you can descend a 250-foot-high cliff.

Another way of rappelling which is often used is to put a sling under your legs and attach a carabiner to it. The sling is made in the form of a loop out of 7⁄16-inch nylon rope. It should be just large enough so that you can make a figure eight out of it. One leg goes into each hole. The carabiner is attached to the middle of it, and the rappel rope is placed through the carabiner, goes up over the right shouder, and is held by the left hand and lightly held by the right hand. Everything is like the body rappel method described except that the rope goes through the carabiner on the figure-eight loop rather than under your leg. If you ever use this method, do not take an extra turn of rope around the carabiner. It is true that such a turn will take friction away from your body and help with any possible rope burns, but it can get snarled.

There are on the market various brake bars and descending rings, but a beginner should not use them at first. There are reports of them snarling. The rings are not as strong as carabiners. Anyway, a beginner should learn for his own safety and for the safety of others how to rappel with *just* a rope.

Rappelling is used primarily to get down cliffs after a climb is over. However, there are times when it is used for exploring future routes or for checking strange rock formations. A man who has rappelled a hundred feet down a cliff, for example, can quite easily "walk" back and forth on the cliff for some distance as the rappel rope acts like a pendulum. Thus a climber can occasionally use it to investigate things.

After rappelling, be sure to pull the rope carefully out of the piton eye. Try to keep it from twisting. If it is stuck, do not try to climb back up it. It may suddenly give and you will fall. Because ropes sometimes are difficult to pull through a piton eye, it is sometimes best to make a sling and put it through the eye. The rope sling can be nylon, because the rope is not going to be sliding through it when there is any weight on the rope. While a person is rappelling, the ropes will not be rubbing together. A rope pulled gently through the sling will not produce enough heat for any danger.

You may wonder at this point whether or not the piton is left up above the climbers. Yes, it is. But it is still cheaper than the price of a movie ticket. If you come across an old piton at a good rappelling point, you can check it. If it is in good condition, you can use it again, but never use an old sling.

It is often very helpful in planning a rock climb to have a system whereby you can with some objectivity describe various climbing routes in terms of their difficulties. Several systems have been devised, but none is really perfect. The following one, I think, is as good as any.

Grade 1. Technically, this is the easiest climb of all. You can go up a cliff graded 1 and keep your hands in your pockets all the way up. You never have to touch the rocks.

Grade 2. A person on a grade-2 climb will need to grasp the rocks. An analogy might be that of climbing a ladder. All the handholds and footholds, however, are easy, and the average person will understand them all. A rope is almost never used on such a climb. However, if there is a drop-off or the climbers are on a very steep cliff, a rope might be needed.

Grade 3. This is very much like a grade-2 climb except that the handholds and footholds are more complex and the climber must learn how to use them. Some thinking will be needed to know exactly how to place the hands and feet and how to move from one secure place to the next. Expert climbers might not rope up for such a place. Everyone else, however, would rope up.

Grade 4. On this climb pitons will be used for belays and possibly for running belays. In such a climb there are dangers from the type of handholds and footholds used or from the nature of the rock. This is a technical climb requiring an expert knowledge of climbing, at least from the leader.

Grade 5. This climb calls for tension climbing. It is impossible without direct aid. On this climb, however, the cliff will have natural cracks where you can pound in pitons.

Grade 6. On this type of climb you will need drills and expansion bolts, as there will be no natural crack.

Grade 7. This is a theoretically impossible climb. You will be faced with cliffs which are too steep to climb, and which will not hold equipment. An absolutely sheer cliff of very soft or rotten rock might qualify.

I would recommend that any climber try out each grade, going from 1 to 2, 3, 4, and 5 in sequence without skipping any grade. Indeed, you should really be quite expert in one grade before attempting the next.

Of course, the grades refer to dry rock only. Snow and ice can literally change a grade-1 climb to a grade-5 climb. Very few large cliffs are the same grade from bottom to top. In judging a cliff, give it a grade for its most difficult stretch.

Almost all mountain clubs or outing groups will carefully describe the route they plan to take so that members and guests will know ahead of time what sort of climb it will be. When asked to go on a rock climb, always ask what type of a climb it will be.

18

How to Climb on Ice and Snow

As most mountains are covered with snow and ice, a climber must know how to deal with both. The techniques used on snow and ice differ in several ways from those used on rock. In many ways they are more demanding, as both snow and ice are treacherous and more accidents occur on them than on rocks. Get an expert to teach you.

Many mountains are bordered by glaciers, and there are interesting summits which you can reach only by crossing a glacier. Thus, you should know how to cross one safely. But to do so you need to know how they move and act. Glaciers are moving rivers of ice. In many high mountains snow never melts, but gets deeper and deeper each year, and, at the same time more compact until it turns to ice, which after a while starts sliding slowly downhill. Like all rivers, glaciers head for the ocean. In the Arctic and Antarctic regions they reach it. In most areas of the world as glaciers reach lower altitudes, higher summer temperatures melt them.

Water can flow more or less smoothly, but ice, being a solid, cannot. As a glacier moves along, usually at a rate of only a few feet a day, the ice keeps breaking. For example, as a glacier goes over a rise, the ice cannot conform to the shape, so it splits open. When the glacier goes over a dip the breaks are pushed together and the ice solidifies once more. The cracks in the ice are called crevasses. Some are small, but others are large and can reach depths of a hundred feet or more. Crevasses present a problem to climbers. First the crevasses which appear in a glacier one week will be gone the next. Old ones

Two climbers going into the snow- and glacier-covered mountains of Switzerland. (*Courtesy Swiss National Tourist Office*)

will close and new ones appear. Thus, there is no way of mapping the crevasses of a glacier. Each time climbers cross a glacier they must explore it for themselves.

This can be very difficult. Often the crevasses can crisscross a glacier in chaotic patterns. In general, the patterns are such that most crevasses cross a glacier at right angles to its flow, while others caused by pressure on the sides move parallel to the flow of the glacier. Further, like rivers with tributaries, many glaciers are met by others. A confused landscape of crevasses, pinnacles of ice, broken blocks of snow, even rivers of water can be found where they meet. The climber is in a maze and can be confused as to where to go. Perhaps worse than that is the fact that snow blowing across glaciers will frequently hide crevasses. This is, of course, a great danger, as you may walk on the snow and think that you are standing on firm ice, not aware at all that you are standing on a snow-covered crevasse and that in a second you will plunge through the snow into an abyss.

The highest point and source of a glacier is called

A typical mountain glacier. The deep cracks are called crevasses. Climbers crossing the glacier would have to be careful of them. It would also be tricky to choose a good route across such a glacier, but it is all part of the sport of mountain climbing. (*Courtesy Swiss National Tourist Office*)

the head, and its lowest point is called the foot. Like a river, the left bank of a glacier is on its left side as you face in the direction of its flow.

Some areas of a glacier tend to be more dangerous and chaotic than others. The foot of a glacier is dangerous. Ice pinnacles and other chunks of ice break away at the foot. If a glacier reaches the sea, icebergs, some as long as a hundred miles, break away. Imagine the force of such a break. The foot of a glacier usually has deep crevasses which are extremely unstable.

Crevasses are usually quite difficult where a glacier goes over a rise, or goes over a giant steplike ledge. A glacier which is squeezing through a narrow canyon can also be quite difficult. Glaciers frequently shrink away from cliffs, leaving a deep canyonlike gap between the glacier and the cliff.

Glaciers are least confusing where they flow along over a smooth gentle slope—that is, one without rises, dips, or any other sudden change in the direction of the slope. The more uniform the surface under a glacier the more uniform the top of the glacier will be.

Before crossing a glacier it is best to get information about it from local mountain climbers. It is also wise to make an exploratory trip, if possible, along mountain ridges bordering the glacier. Get up on one and look down over the glacier and try to determine the best route across it, either where there are few difficult crevasses or where the crevasses are parallel and uniform. Even difficult crevasses can be negotiated if you know that they all have a parallel pattern, or other logical, easily remembered patterns.

If you are in a wilderness area and must cross a large glacier, it is often best to collect beforehand willow or similar branches. When crossing the glacier, mark your route with the branches. They will make it much easier to return across the glacier, if you come back over it a few days later. Be sure the branches are placed so that if you stand next to any one branch, you can easily see the next one in line, even in an average snowstorm.

When a party of climbers crosses a glacier, all members rope together. No fewer than three climbers together should cross a glacier. A larger party is better. All should carry ice axes, have on crampons, and wear goggles and, of course, warm clothing. A nylon rope of one inch in

A deep crevasse. Notice the snow and ice bridge. Sometimes snow can completely cover a crevasse, and an unwary climber may not even see it and fall in. In addition, even sturdy-looking bridges can suddenly fall in. (*Courtesy the American Alpine Club*)

A close-up of a chaotic landscape such as is often found on large glaciers. A climber must try to avoid such places or know how to get through them. (*Courtesy Swiss National Tourist Office*)

diameter should be taken. It should be at least one hundred feet long.

The leader of the party should go first, at each step of the way probing with the shaft of his ice axe for crevasses. By pushing the axe down into the snow, he can feel if solid ice is beneath. If there is snow covering a hidden crevasse, he will be able to feel it. While the leader is moving forward, the other members of the party have him on belay.

The party should cross a glacier in formation. If they are walking parallel to crevasses, the group should form a zigzag line. The reason for the zigzag line is that if one falls into a crevasse, the others can help. Do not get into a single file. Do not bunch up together in a small group. Keep as distant from one another as reasonably possible. The rope should be rather taut between each two people.

If the party is walking at right angles to the general direction of the crevasses, the party then walks single file. Thus, if the leader or anyone else falls into a hidden crevasse, the others will be above it on solid ice.

It is possible to leap across some small crevasses. Before you ever do so, be absolutely sure you will get all the way across. When you leap across a crevasse, you will first coil up the rope between you and the person behind. When you jump, release the coil while in midair. This prevents the rope from stopping you. Always be sure to

A party of climbers crossing a large glacier. (*Courtesy Swiss National Tourist Office*)

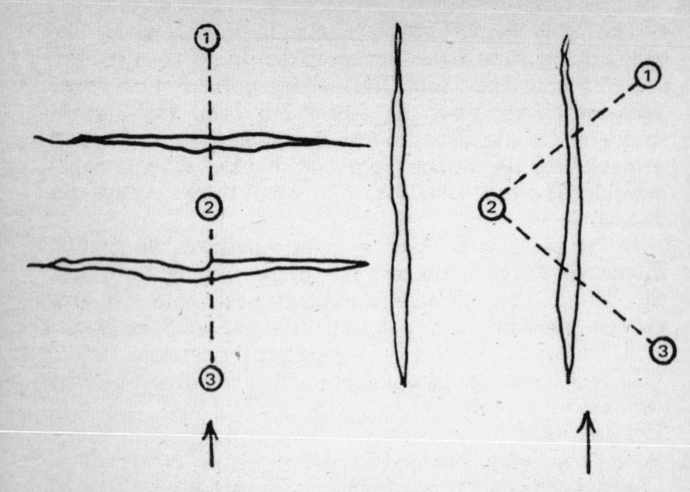

The correct party formation for crossing a glacier. Most crevasses form more or less in parallel lines. If the party is crossing at right angles to the crevasses, they should walk as shown in the left illustration. If they are walking parallel to the crevasses, they should walk as shown in the right illustration.

have more than enough slack so the rope does not jerk you downward into the crevasse.

When you jump, the ice axe is held parallel to the ground. The spike points to the right and the head to the left. The pick is held downward and away from the body. The ice axe is grasped in both hands. It is held so that you will not land with the spike toward you, and not in a way that you could land on the head of the axe. If you land and start to fall, you can shift the ice axe to the left so that when you fall, you will fall on the shaft and not on any sharp edges.

If a person falls into a crevasse, the rest of the party must quickly do all they can to facilitate the rescue. Speed is of the greatest importance. It is often so cold in a crevasse that you begin to suffer right away. The cold temperatures, especially if there is water there, can chill you so much that you will lose consciousness within a short period of time. Death can follow soon afterward.

If a leader on belay falls into a crevasse it is often

possible for the rest of the party to pull him out by bodily force. They must take the precaution of seeing that the rope does not dig into the lip of the crevasse. To keep it from doing so, place an ice axe shaft under the rope where it might dig in. Even if the leader cannot be directly pulled out, he might be able to help by "walking" up the side of the crevasse with his crampons while the rest of the people pull on the rope.

If that fails, and the leader is conscious, the party should lower the inch-thick nylon rope. With it, he can use prusik knots. Each person, before going on any glacier, will know beforehand how to use prusik knots.

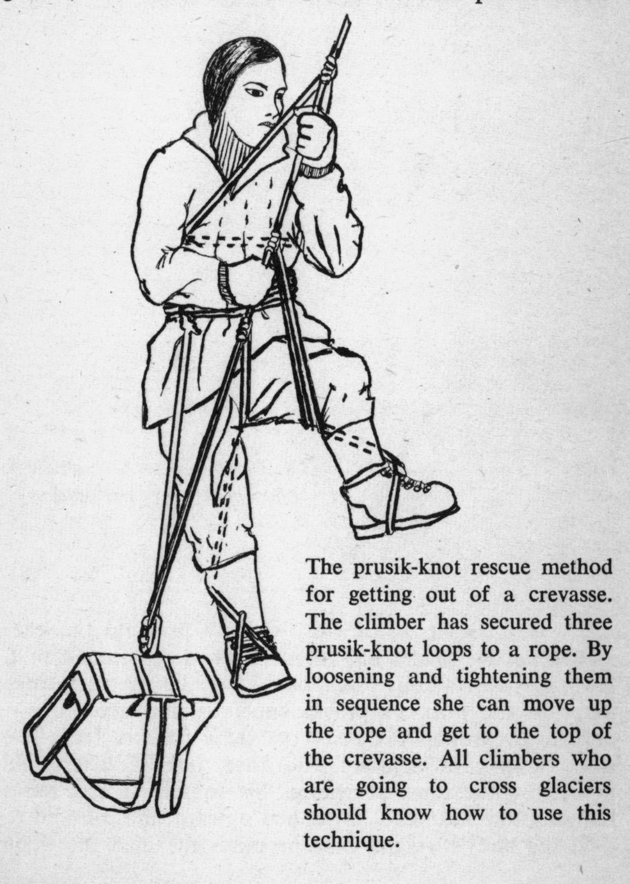

The prusik-knot rescue method for getting out of a crevasse. The climber has secured three prusik-knot loops to a rope. By loosening and tightening them in sequence she can move up the rope and get to the top of the crevasse. All climbers who are going to cross glaciers should know how to use this technique.

The one-inch rope is used, as it is far easier to work a prusik knot on it than on smaller ropes, which stretch too much. The rope is secured on the ice by an ice axe. Be sure that the ice axe is deeply embedded into the ice and that it goes straight down into it. To help secure the rope, other climbers can also hold it behind the ice axe, giving it extra support.

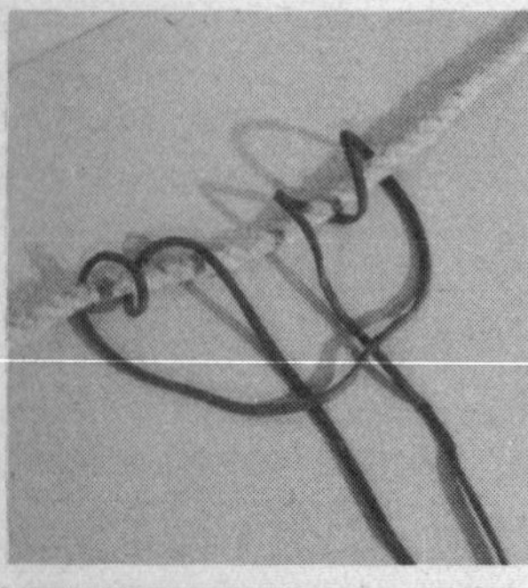

The prusik knot. (*Photograph by the author*)

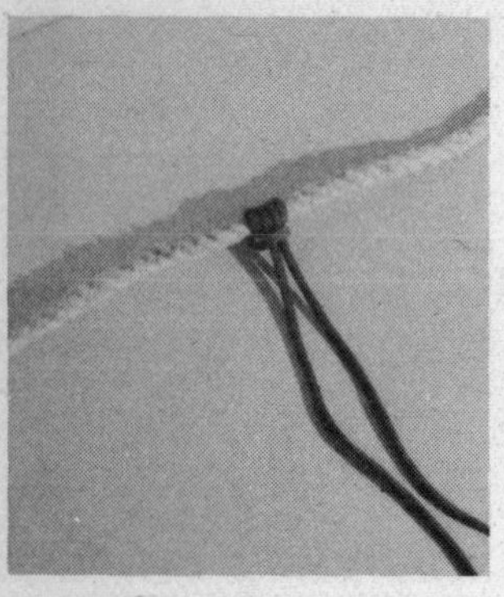

The prusik knot tightened. (*Photograph by the author*)

The climber in the crevasse quickly ties into the one-inch rope. He places his knapsack on it to keep it taut. He also takes off his crampons. Next, he attaches three loops in the form of prusik knots to the large rope—one to go around his body and two for his feet. The three loops are adjusted and then one is taken and moved up the rope. He places his foot in it and raises himself. The next knot is pushed upward and allowed to hold the body's weight; then he raises the next foot loop up and puts weight on it, raising himself again. The process is repeated until he gains the top of the crevasse.

The gergli method is another way to make a rescue from a crevasse. In this method you either use two ropes or tie into the middle of a rope. Place the two ropes under a loop of rope around your chest. Then make loops tied with figure-eight knots for your feet. After taking off your crampons, place your feet in the loops. Be sure that the ropes go around your legs, for that arrangement holds them in and your feet will not slip out of the loops. Put your weight on one loop, which is on a rope attached to an ice axe above the crevasse by prusik knots. Raise yourself and put all your weight on the loop. Next, raise your other foot. That loop is pulled up by the climbers on top of the glacier. When it is up about a foot and a half, it is secured and you put your weight on that foot and raise yourself. The process is repeated until you are out of the crevasse.

Today many climbers carry nylon pulleys with them, which are attachable to carabiners. A rope can be passed from the person who has fallen, through a pulley, and back down to another pulley and then up again. Climbers can then pull the person directly out of the crevasse. The mechanical advantage is such that they will pull only one third the weight and still lift him.

To attach it, the climbers on the top of the glacier put the rope through a pulley and carabiner and attach another pulley and carabiner to the rope and lower it on the rope down to the person, who attaches the carabiner to himself and sees to it that the rope moves freely through the pulley arrangement.

If a climber falls into a crevasse and is injured, another climber will have to go quickly down into the crevasse and aid him. The climber sees to it that the injured climber is right side up and not hanging head downward. The healthy climber moves upward on a prusik-knot arrangement. He constantly lifts the other climber in such a way that some slack is gained in the injured climber's rope. The person above takes up the slack, tightening it and holding it around an ice axe. The healthy climber moves up, once more lifting the injured climber as much as possible, once more getting slack, which is taken up, and so on.

It cannot be stressed how important it is that all of

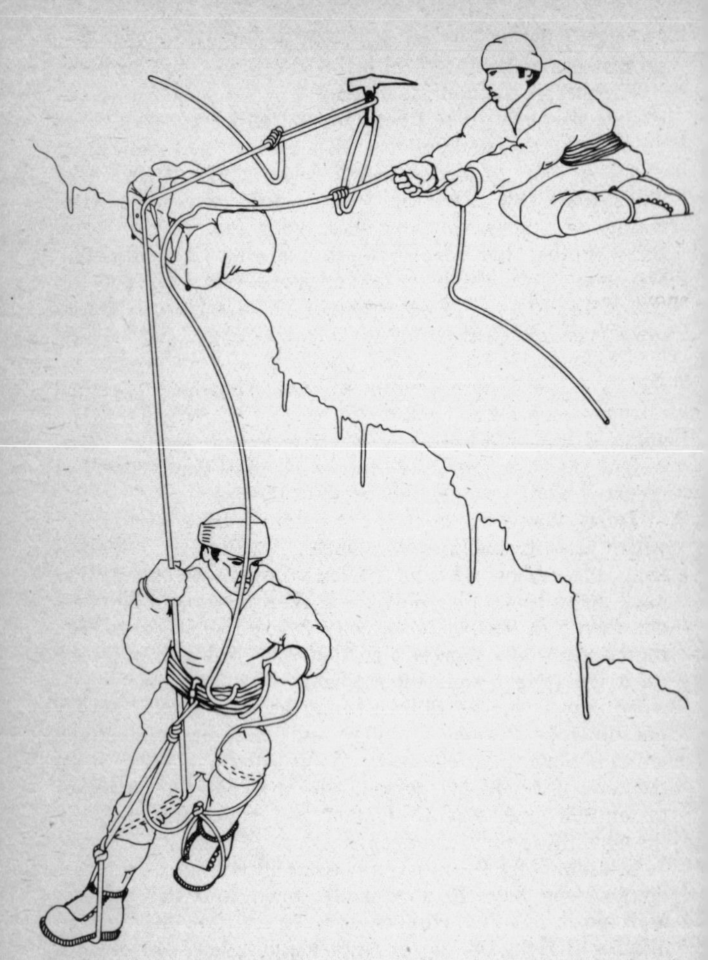

The gergli method for getting out of a crevasse. The method requires two people. The man at the top is loosening and tightening prusik knots. The tightened one is holding the climber, who is raising his left foot. The man above will pull on the rope and then tighten up the prusik knot so that the climber can shift his weight to his left-hand rope and thus take another step upward. Proceeding in this way step by step, he can reach the top of the crevasse and be out of it.

these rescue techniques be practiced before you ever go on a glacier. They should be learned so that they become second nature.

Fortunately, crevasse accidents are not too common. Indeed you may go across glaciers every week of your life without ever having to make a rescue. On the other hand, you must be prepared for an emergency.

Snow and ice conditions vary a great deal. On any given slope there can be all sorts of different varieties of snow and ice. At times a slope might be bare and free of snow. It might be deep in snow, covered with ice, ready to avalanche, or have on it snow which is hard or snow which is soft. It is the changing nature of snow and ice which makes them both so difficult and so dangerous.

It is good to know of various snow and ice conditions, and the following terms describe many of the types you will encounter.

POWDER SNOW. In high, extremely cold mountain areas, snow will fall which looks and acts something like dry dust. The separate crystals stay hard due to the cold temperature. In addition, they do not cling to each other. After a snowfall, powder snow lies in heaps of loose snow. Skiers love to ski through such snow, but climbers can have trouble with powder snow as they tend to sink deep down into it. No one ever sinks out of sight in it no matter how deep it is, but it can be waist deep and stop you. Furthermore, powder snow must be watched, as a wind can raise it and blow it about, so that you think that you are in a blizzard.

SNOW CRUSTS. Most of the snow that falls in the mountains is powder snow. Eventually a crust forms on it. Crusts form in three ways. A wind crust is formed when a prevailing wind packs the snow. After a while, under the constant pressure of the wind plus some melting, a crust is formed. Another type of crust is formed by the melting of the top of the snow. This usually happens when the sun hits it. The warm rays will make the top snowflakes begin to melt and settle. Another way it can happen is that warm air above the freezing point will move over the snow, melting it. Crusts can be paper thin or a few inches thick. If they are thick enough, it is usually easy to walk on top of the snow. It can support your weight and you can walk for miles on it without ever falling through the crust. On the other hand, the crust may be so thin that you do fall through into deeper powder snow underneath.

You often have reason to look at distant snow and determine if it is powder snow or snow with a crust. Powder snow does not glint in sunlight. It even looks powdery. Wind crust usually looks chalky, but not powdery. Crust which has been formed by melting often has a shiny, though not necessarily smooth, surface. In certain light conditions it looks sort of glassy. A climber must learn how to judge snow conditions as well as possible from a distance. If you can find snow which has a good crust, you may find an easy route to some distant location.

One of the worst conditions is found when clear, hard ice covers rock slopes. This can happen when cold rains fall on rocks which are already below the freezing point. The rain hits the rocks, and ice forms all over them. When that happens, even the best handholds and footholds become nearly impossible to use. Such conditions are extremely treacherous. Ice can also form, and frequently does, when higher slopes are in sunlight and lower slopes are in shadow. The sunlight will melt snow and ice higher up, and water will flow down from the higher places and move across cold rocks and freeze into solid clear ice. Always avoid such areas.

Ice can form on top of snow as well. Water from higher slopes can flow across a snow crust and freeze into solid ice. Quite often you can kick through such ice and get a foothold in the snow itself, or you can cut steps in it with an ice axe. On the other hand such ice can be so deep that you cannot cut all the way through it. If so, it is wise to avoid it.

A treacherous condition exists when there is a layer of ice on the ground and powder snow falls on top of it. You may look at such snow and think that it is safe, but actually such snow can easily slide downhill over the ice. Worse yet is when powder snow lying on ice has a hard crust of snow on top of it. On viewing it you may very well think it is snow that can be trusted. Yet the crust will slide over the powder snow, which in turn can slide on the ice. You could find powder snow with a crust overlaid with solid ice, or a crust overlaid with powder snow. It is obvious that there can be all sorts of combinations of ice and snow.

Snow on any slope will tend to slip downhill, depending on various conditions. In general, snow will tend to slip on steep slopes. As a matter of fact, snow rarely clings to slopes steeper than about sixty degrees. The smoother the surface under the snow, the more easily it will slip. Snow on top of ice can move away more easily. Snow on top of a uniform slope can move away more easily than snow which lies on uneven ground. If the ground under the snow has many rocks and boulders, it may not slip downhill at all.

The condition of the snow itself will matter. Powder snow can move easily. Old snow which has packed down is more stable. Slush can also move relatively easily.

The temperature of both the air and rocks under the snow can affect its nature. For example, if the ground under snow is warming up, the snow touching that ground may actually be melting, no matter what the surface of the snow looks like. If it is melting, water may be lying between the snow and ground. If so, the snow may easily slide downhill on the layer of water. This is one reason why springtime is a time of many avalanches. On the other hand, if the ground has warmed up and melted the snow and then cooled down again to a temperature below freezing, the resulting ice will make the snow cling more tightly to the rocks. If the air temperature or ground temperature is above freezing for a long enough time, the whole snow mass may melt internally. The snow will then sag and lose all of its powderiness. The whole mass will be relatively compact.

All of this may sound complex, and it is. It takes practice to understand snow. Even the best mountain climbers have on occasion misjudged it. Thus the only thing one can say is make the attempt. Probe with the ice axe. Try to determine what the snow is lying on. Do not put too much trust in snow conditions. Always play it safe and decide that snow will not give away its secrets easily. Distrust snow most after a heavy snowfall, during times of temperature changes, and during the springtime. Snow is at its best, which is not saying much, after a long period of stable weather when there have been no snowfalls for at least a week.

An avalanche falling down the cliffs of a large mountain. Climbers must always study a mountain and determine where avalanches may fall. Not all come from such steep cliffs by any means. Many start on gentle slopes. In the picture notice that the avalanche is falling in a depression. Note also that forests at the base of the mountain have been slashed by past avalanches. Such destruction of trees is a sure sign that avalanches have occurred there. (*Courtesy Swiss National Tourist Office*)

You should never cross snow which might avalanche nor cross beneath slopes which have avalanche danger. On the other hand, since any snow on any slope might slip down and form an avalanche, you must know what is safest to do.

Look over a snow field and, if you think it might avalanche, stay away from it. If you think it is stable but that there is any chance at all that it might avalanche, then take the following precautions.

Do not traverse such a snow field. It is safer to go directly up it, single file, each person trying to step in the footprints of the leader. This disturbs the snow less than if the party crosses the snow field. The party can keep climbing until it is at the top of the field and cross it there.

If a party comes to a snow field which looks risky and they absolutely have no choice but to cross it, the leader starts across. He is given a long lead of rope. He crosses the snow field alone and tries to get completely across it to the opposite side. Often a party can count on some luck, so that the leader can probably get to a firm outcrop or firm place. The next person follows in the leader's footprints, careful all the time not to disturb the snow. Each member crosses alone tied on to as long a section of rope as possible.

If the leader crosses as far as possible but has not gotten to a rock outcrop or firm place, he will push the ice axe into the snow up to its head and belay the next person with it.

Avalanche cord is long, colored cord, usually red or orange. Wear a long cord about fifty feet in length. If an avalanche occurs and you are buried, the cord, hopefully, will still be above the snow. Thus others looking for you can find you quickly and dig you out.

There are small radios on the market which give out a steady beep. People crossing dangerous places keep their radios on "send." The radios can also be switched to receive. Thus if someone in the party is buried under the snow, the other members of the party can switch their radios to "receive." As the rescuers get nearer to the buried person, the beeps become louder and the buried person can be found.

Such rescues after the accident are not as effective by any means as prevention. Do not go into avalanche regions when there is any danger. If there is danger, climb on rock or on ridges.

In snow, you cut steps with the adze side of the axe. You raise the ice axe up and bring it down and the adze cuts out a chunk of snow. Do not swing your shoulders much, as you could lose balance. In cutting steps, let the weight of the ice axe do most of the work.

Always be sure that the first cut is near you, the next farther away, and so forth. Cut two steps so as not to waste time. Be sure that every step is long enough to accommodate your foot.

At times you may be on such a steep slope that you will also be cutting handholds with your ice axe. Be sure that they slope downward and are deep enough so that you can easily get a grip on them.

Because of the tiring nature of the work, it is best not to use the ice axe at all. If you can, it is better to kick footholds in the snow. Though it may sound more tiring, it is actually less so. Also, because of the exertion, it is always best for all the members of the party to take turns cutting steps.

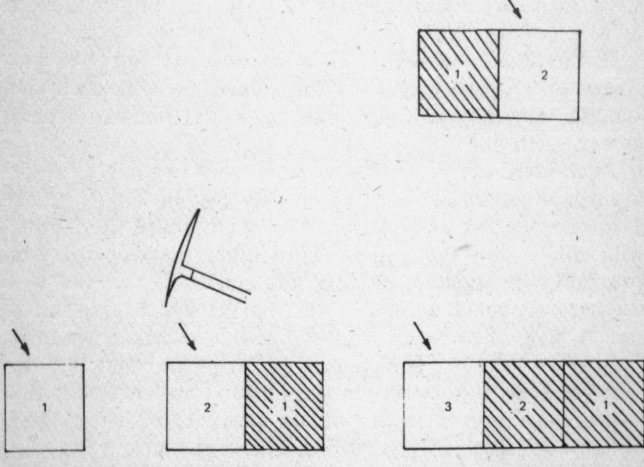

The correct way to cut steps with an ice axe. Always cut the step nearest you (the shaded area) first. This procedure saves energy. Also you can more easily make the steps and clean them out.

The correct way to use crampons on a steep slope. Note that the feet are turned in such a way that every single point on the man's crampons is gripping the snow. Note too that he is also using his ice axe as an extra point to grip the slope.

On most slopes it is easiest to go up in a zigzag pattern. It takes less energy to climb a slope if you angle up it rather than go straight up it. The most comfortable angle should be sought. Except on slopes where there is avalanche danger, it is best not to go straight up the slope. If someone falls at such a time, he may fall on someone directly below. Even if there is no such danger, it is easier to cut zigzag steps. Snow does not keep falling on the lower members of the party.

You should put on crampons when you are on any snow or ice conditions which seem risky. Also, it is always best to put them on *before* they are needed. Do not walk on rocks with them, however, or the points will be dulled, if not damaged.

There are times when you may very well want them even if you are crossing level countryside.

On steep slopes you have to know how to use crampons. It should be obvious that the more points you have sticking into the snow, the more of a grip you will have on it. Note how the ankles and feet are turned in the illustration. Notice also that the climber is on a slope so steep that he has the pick of his ice axe into the snow to help hold him. You should practice this way of standing on a steep snow slope some place where you are perfectly safe before ever trying it on a cliff high in the mountains.

You will also want to learn how to turn. The way a climber turns and goes in the opposite direction—on a zigzag path, for instance—is as follows. One foot is facing directly ahead. As you turn, stand so that both feet are pointing forward and all of the crampon points are into the snow. As you will then be standing more upright, you will drive the spike of your ice axe into the cliff. Next, face into the cliff and point your right foot to the right and your left foot to the left. Once more, keep all points in the snow. Pushing against the ice axe, turn so that both feet are pointing in the direction you wish to go. Next, arrange your feet as shown in the illustration, with one foot down and the ankle turned.

Crampons often ball up with snow, especially if the snow is wet. Knock the snow off with the spike of the

The correct way to stop a fall on snow. The climber is using the pick end of the axe's head to dig into the snow. The adze is up into his shoulder. He can place his weight on it. He is slowly but steadily pushing the pick into the snow so that it will grip. Notice how he keeps the spike at the end of the ice axe up so that it cannot get jabbed into the snow. If it did, it could stop him so quickly that he would somersault over backward. He is putting his feet into the snow to help stop his fall. However, if he had crampons on, he would hold his feet up, so that they could not grip the snow and throw him. All climbers should know how to do this and practice it on safe snow slopes.

ice axe. Be sure to keep the points free of snow so that they can do their job of jabbing and gripping.

One of the big reasons for carrying an ice axe is to use it in case you fall on snow or ice. In such a case, the ice axe can help stop your fall.

If you are walking along on a steep snow or ice slope and fall, do the following immediately. Lie on your stomach. Put your ice axe under your arms as shown in the illustration. Push slowly down but forcefully on the head of the ice axe so that the pick end is digging into the snow. Even as you get onto your stomach, be sure that your feet are held up off the icy slope, especially if you have on crampons. If the crampons ever dig into the snow, your feet will come to a sudden stop and you will somersault right over them with possibly fatal results. Once you get the pick end of your ice axe into the snow, you will come to a halt.

This maneuver is extremely important to know, for it has saved many climbers' lives. Indeed, all beginners should practice it on snowy but safe slopes. Every split second counts, for the more quickly you can get the pick into the snow and put pressure on it, the more quickly you can stop your fall.

There are several ways of belaying while climbing on snow and ice. In general the belays are not as good as those on rocks, as snow and ice do not give the belayer as much security as solid rock does.

One commonly used method of belaying a person on hard snow is to use an ice axe as a secure point for a belay. The technique is simple. Take an ice axe and push the shaft down into the snow, so that only the head of the ice axe is sticking above the snow. Most ice axes

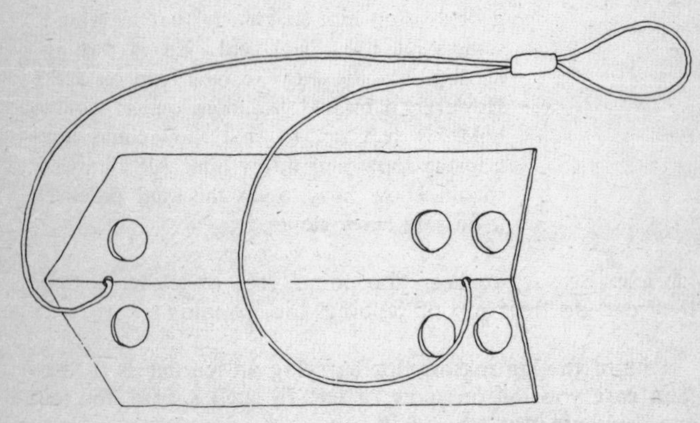

The deadman or snow fluke. Place the blade downward into the snow and attach a carabiner to the wire. The pull against it will make it dig deeper into the snow. It will hold better than an ice axe for a snow belay.

today have an eye in the head to which you can attach a rope and carabiner. The belayer, if above or below the other climber, stands in front of the ice axe and gives the climber a hip belay or shoulder belay. The ice axe thus secures the belayer. Usually the belayer ties into the carabiner with a figure-eight knot tied into a loop. This belay is never as strong as those found on rocks, but it will do and has saved people who have fallen on snow.

A more secure belay is obtained if the belayer uses a "deadman," which is a snow anchor. It is a metal plate with one end cut in a V shape. In the plate are eyelets, and two wire cables that end in a secured loop are attached to them. Attach a carabiner to the wire loop. The advantage of using the deadman is that when pressure is put on it, it tends to be pushed deeper into the snow, where it has more and more holding power. Thus, it is much more secure than an ice axe.

For ice work one can use ice pitons for a belay.

19

Mountain Rescues, Emergencies, First Aid

Mountain rescue work is really a subject for expert mountain climbers, and as such is beyond the scope of an introductory book on mountain climbing. Beginners, however, should know a few things about mountain rescue work, as it can be of tremendous importance to them.

First of all, beginners should know that there are groups who are prepared to aid climbers. For example, in mountainous national parks and national monuments, the rangers are quite frequently trained to help injured or stranded mountain climbers. Some cities, such as Boulder, Colorado, have groups which can rescue mountain climbers who need their help. In most mountain clubs there are groups who know how to carry out mountain rescue work.

Thus, when you go climbing in a mountainous region, there is a good chance that there will be some group nearby who can rescue you and your companions if the need arises. Before you go on a climb, find out who those people are and how you can get in touch with them. Also, it is wise for you to tell your friends how to get in touch with them. Leave names, addresses, and telephone numbers with your friends or family. Then if you are late in returning, your friends can contact the qualified mountain climbers who will help you. *Before* is the key word. In the event of an accident you do not want to waste time looking for help; you want to know exactly where to go for it. Furthermore, if you and your party are all stuck together someplace, there will be no way of reaching help. It must be done for you by others who realize that you are overdue in returning.

If you are climbing and there is an accident in which anyone is injured, first of all try to determine the nature of the injuries. If the person is bleeding, try to stop it immediately. Determine, if you can, what bones are broken. Be especially careful to see if there have been any injuries to the spine. If the person complains of back pains or cannot move his legs, then he may have a spinal injury. If so, do not move him, unless it will cost him his life (or someone else's) to leave him.

After checking out the extent of injuries, make every effort to keep the patient warm. Cover him immediately with warm clothes, or, better yet, get him into a warm sleeping bag away from the wind.

Sometimes it may be necessary for an injured person to be left while you go for help. For example, if two people are climbing together and one falls, the other will have to go and get help. If three are climbing together and one is injured, the other two may have to go and get help together, because of the nature of the climb.

If the person is conscious, discuss his needs. Try to do everything possible to make him warm and comfortable. Give the person some food and water. Tell him where you are going and whom you will contact. If the person is unconscious, be absolutely sure that he is secured to the cliff. If needed, place a piton in the cliff and secure the person to it by ropes. If the person is unconscious and is left, write down all that you are doing. Leave available food, medicine, and water. You can imagine how disconcerting it would be to come to and find yourself alone and hurt in the mountains.

Before leaving anyone, be sure that you mark the spot carefully. This is extremely important. If you mark the spot with a jacket which is visible for a distance or with some other highly visible object, the rescue party, which may move much faster than you can, will be able quickly and easily to find the injured climber. In addition, it is possible for a climber, especially under stress, not to recall exactly where the injured person is located.

After doing all you can for the injured person, be extra careful that you yourself do not become injured. The trouble is that those going for help will often be nervous and wish to hurry along faster than they should. Such conditions make it possible for them to make a mistake. It hardly needs to be pointed out what a disaster it would be if they in turn were injured with little or no hope of anyone getting rescued quickly. Make all attempts to stay calm. Be careful in choosing a safe route back to help. You must sometimes choose a longer route than a short route, because it will be safer for you to do so.

There are times, of course, when the injured person need not be left alone. If the party has more than two climbers, someone should stay while the others go for help.

Most of the time the injured person can be carried off the mountain or to a better location, such as to a nearby cabin.

If a person is to be moved, it is best to carry him in a stretcher. Of course, climbers will not be carrying a stretcher with them. However, if you have a climbing rope, you can quickly make a rope stretcher from it. The illustration shows how it is done. Long before going on a mountain climbing trip it would be worthwhile to practice making such a stretcher. It only takes a few minutes to make. Notice that it is made up of only two kinds of knots. One is the overhand knot made in a loop. The other knot, connecting the loops to the other half of the rope, is tied as illustrated. Thus, if you have a rope with you, you also always have a stretcher.

Another type of stretcher can be made with two poles

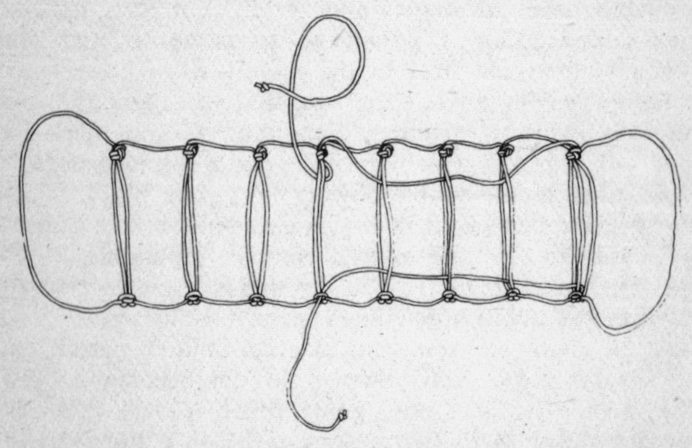

An emergency stretcher which climbers can easily make from a rope.

Figure-eight knot in a loop. In the stretcher the loop would be longer. (*Photograph by the author*)

The knot used in the rope stretcher to secure the end of the loop. (*Photograph by the author*)

and coats. Get the poles from the forest. They should be free of branches and at least 1½ inches in diameter. Turn the coats inside out, and button or zipper them shut with the sleeves on the *inside*. Place them on the ground and run the poles through the sleeves. One pole goes through the right sleeve and the other pole through the left. Two or three coats are needed. Place the injured person on the back part of the coats.

First aid is not really part of this book for the simple reason that there are many good books about it available. In fact, every mountain climber should learn first aid techniques before going into the mountains. There are also many courses open to the public. You can find out about them through the YMCA, Boy Scouts, or through your family doctor. On many hikes it is not unreasonable, in terms of weight, to carry a small first aid book along.

But there are some aspects of first aid which should be mentioned. First of all, mountain climbers should carry a first aid kit. The big question is what should be in it? I do not think there is *one* answer to that question. Therefore, we should approach it according to possible needs. Needs vary a great deal. For example, if you are winter camping in the Rockies where the temperature is never going to be above freezing, you would hardly need anything for snake bites or insect bites. The best way to approach the subject would be to guess what is most likely to go wrong first and work on from there. Let us do that.

Blisters are always a possibility. Therefore, take along some moleskin and some scissors to cut it.

The next most common injury is probably minor cuts, slivers, and burns. For them take along Band-Aids, tweezers for pulling the slivers out, a small tube of burn ointment, and a small tube of an antiseptic, such as Bacitracin.

A severe sprained ankle really stops a trip for a person, but occasionally you may get minor ones. An Ace bandage is very handy. It is a stretchable bandage that comes in a long roll (you never cut the bandage, you use the whole roll). When you put it on a minor sprained ankle, it holds the ankle in place. With the bandage are little clasps to hold it on. When you buy the bandage, open up the box and see that the clasps are with it.

In warm weather take along a snake-bite kit. The kit comes with everything needed, plus, usually, a set of instructions on how to use it. Rock climbers must always be aware of snakes, as they frequently live on and in just the rocks you may wish to climb. Also they have the bad habit of sunning themselves on rock ledges just where you may put your hand. Luckily, snake bites are a rarity.

One might get a worse cut than a knick, or a burn that is more than a small spot that gets red from heat. Take along sterile gauze pads three by three inches square. With them you will need a roll of one-inch adhesive tape. Get a roll about five yards in length (the package will give this information on it).

Before going into an area, try to determine whether or not it will be worth your while to carry an insect repellent. If you have any doubts, carry it along.

Some people suffer from constipation on a trip that lasts several days. A chewy laxative might make you feel better.

Many people get headaches on mountain trips. And most people get aching muscles. So take aspirin.

Salt tablets are a must. They replace the salt lost through sweating, and they cut down on thirst. Some people keep drinking water in an effort to replace lost minerals and salt. One or two salt tablets will help the system retain water, and can help a great deal to keep you from suffering from sore and aching muscles. Of course, never overdo it with salt tablets or you'll be as thirsty as a camel.

Halazone tablets will kill germs in questionable water. They usually come in small bottles containing a hundred tablets. There will also be directions on the bottle as to how they are used.

Rubbing alcohol is used to put on insect bites to relieve the itching. I personally would probably not bother with it, but it is a "maybe" item. You can sterilize needles with it, but you can do that with a flame, too.

You will need a good cream for stopping the ultraviolet rays of the sunlight. Buy the best you can, as sunburns can be really bad.

Some people suffer from dry skin while in the mountains, and I mean skin which is not necessarily exposed to the direct rays of the sun. Coconut oil is good oil to rub on the skin.

Your lips will crack unless something is done for them. The regular medication sold in most drug stores is not good enough. Get a good salve sold through a mountain goods store, such as Labiosan Lip Salve.

Soap is not part of a first aid kit, but do not forget that you can use it to clean off wounds that are not serious.

Tea is not a first aid item either, but it can be drunk as a stimulant and it also helps settle one's stomach.

Additional medicines might be those for upset stomachs and medicines for allergies, especially if your trip takes you through fields of hay and flowers like goldenrod. If you are going on a long trip, you might ask your doctor to give you a prescription for general antibiotics. Of course, do not forget your regular prescription medicines.

The key to a first aid kit is not so much the things in it, but a good knowledge of first aid. Whatever you take, be sure that the first aid kit is kept clean and that none of the sterile packages get torn. Replace old items. Keep the kit all together in one place.

Before going on some trips it is best to ask your doctor if you need certain shots, such as typhoid and/or cholera, the latter being needed in some countries. Tell him exactly where you will be going so that he can help you.

There are some first aid problems which are uniquely associated with mountain climbing. One of them is frostbite. If your skin gets too cold, it will start to freeze. If too much freezing occurs, it will die. The worse the freezing, the deeper the damage. Unfortunately, the person suffering from frostbite does not feel it. The cold tends to numb the skin.

The first symptom of frostbite is a discoloration of the skin. The skin gets whiter. Frostbite usually occurs first on the extremities such as the ears, nose, fingers, and toes. Climbers should watch each other anytime the temperature is below freezing and there is a wind blowing. The best protection is someone else seeing a part of your skin change color.

If frostbite occurs, take immediate action. Get the affected area warm as quickly as possible. It is an old wives' tale to think that rubbing snow on frostbite will help it. It *will not*. Doing so can cause more damage. Any rubbing of the area is bad. Get something warm on the area, but not something hot.

Snow blindness is an actual blindness. If a person gets snow blindness, there is not much that can be done. Place the person in a dark tent and help protect him from any light. Sometimes, if the temperature is above freezing, cool compresses over the eyes help. Do not do any more. Do not put any medicines at all in his eyes. Rest and darkness are the only cures.

When the internal temperature of a person falls below normal, the person is suffering from hypothermia. The body temperature can go as low as 61 degrees, for example. The obvious cause of hypothermia is that a person simply gets too cold.

All mountain climbers should be able to recognize the symptoms of hypothermia, for it is a very serious condition and can lead to death. A cooling of the body and brain cause the brain to work more slowly and erratically; thus the first symptoms of hypothermia are unusual behavior. There can be a variety of symptoms, but the most usual ones are as follows.

A person may become slow in speech; a common symptom is a slowness in the person's response to a question. You can ask a person who is suffering from hypothermia a question and he will stare at you in sort of a vacant way. Watch for any slowness of mental activities.

There may be trouble with vision, or slurred speech.

On the other hand, a person may have a spurt of energy and go racing along. Violent behavior is another sign of the condition. Some people start cursing and swearing.

An obvious symptom is that the person will complain of the cold or of being too tired. It is sometimes difficult to distinguish this from all the general complaints you might hear all day long. Of course, the person might start shivering. On a beach in the summertime this is not a dangerous symptom, but on a mountain climb, it is.

Anyone who staggers or falls is, of course, obviously suffering and must receive immediate help. The quicker the symptoms are recognized and something is done to help the person, the better. The longer you wait, the more the body will cool down and the longer the recovery will be. And if you wait too long, the person will pass out and the next stage after that is death.

The obvious cure for hypothermia is to warm the person up as quickly as possible. Place him or her immediately into a sleeping bag or a "space blanket." It is wise always to carry a couple of sleeping bags, even on a day trip, if you are facing severe weather with cold temperatures and high winds. A hot-water bottle should be prepared. This is done by placing hot water into a canteen. The person should be given easily digested sugar, and one of the best things is condensed milk (not evaporated milk). If the person's breathing stops, as it may, someone should immediately give him mouth-to-mouth resuscitation. If you must carry the person someplace, be sure to carry him with his head slightly lower than the rest of his body. All the blood possible must get to the brain. If possible, place the person in a sleeping bag with another person for several hours—even for a day.

Sometimes a person who has hypothermia will look dead because the body is working so slowly. If the person looks dead, do not, whatever you do, give up. Continue to try to get him warm. Continue with the artificial respiration.

If the person recovers and looks all right and acts all right, get him off the mountain. It takes several days to recover; until then the person can become ill from it again too easily. Also, the person will be in a weakened condition.

It is important to remember that the condition can occur even in weather where the temperature is above freezing. A few people trapped in weather where the temperature never went below 40 degrees have died of it. It is not the outside temperature that is important but the internal temperature of the body. Even temperatures of 45 degrees can sometimes lower a person's internal temperature to the point of hypothermia.

The phrase "getting lost" can have a wide range of meanings. If you have a knapsack filled with supplies and are lost, you should not give it a thought, for you know that you have food, a sleeping bag, and a map. On the other hand, someone lost in a blizzard on a high peak has to give instant consideration to his problem.

Let us use the term in its more serious meaning. If you are on a high peak in bad weather and you realize you are lost, spend some time thinking about what to do. If you have a map and compass with you, you really will not remain lost. The first thing you should do if you are above timberline is to decide how to get to timberline quickly and safely. There is a big difference in your ability to survive above timberline and below it. Forested areas stop high winds. Tree branches can be used to make some sort of shelter. Wood can be burned. Areas above timberline are wind-swept and often there is virtually no place to escape the wind. There is usually

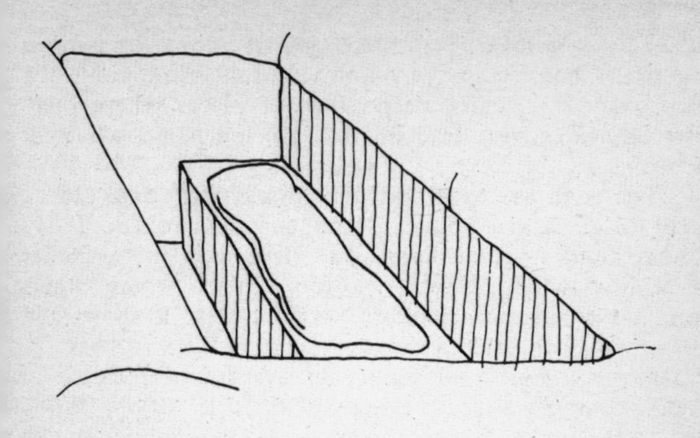

Two views of a snow trench which can be used as an emergency shelter. Dig the trench at right angles to the prevailing wind. A raised snow shelf is left for a sleeping bag. A deeper area into which colder air can seep is dug. It helps make the bed shelf warmer. Tree limbs, skis, or other supports can be placed over the snow trench and covered with twigs, branches, and other materials. Snow is piled on top of all. An entrance is left, and a poncho or other material is used to screen out the wind.

no chance of making a shelter or, of course, making a big fire. Choose your way down to timberline carefully. Stay away from cliffs, deep snow, or places where there may be avalanches. Be deliberate. Do not panic, whatever happens.

When you get to timberline, immediately look for a good place where you can stop and remain for a day or two until someone finds you. First, look for a shelter from high winds. Next, look for a place where others can find you easily. Look for a place near a snow field where you can later place signals.

Once you find a place, try in every way possible to make yourself a cozy camp. Remain in camp. When lost, move only if you are above timberline. Help will eventually be sent, so take it easy.

Sometimes lost persons must camp in the snow. If so, they can sometimes make snow caves. There are several varieties. The simplest to make is to find a big snowdrift made up of rather solid but not dripping-wet snow. Most snowdrifts have a steep side, which you can dig straight into. Snow insulates, and it is often many degrees warmer inside than in the cold wind. Since cold air is heavier than warm air, it is best to slant your tunnel upward. Then when you crawl into the back of it, you will be above the colder air. Be sure that the snowdrift cannot collapse on you. Also make another hole for air so that you won't smother if the tunnel entrance collapses.

A fancier type of snow cave is made like the one just described, except that you tunnel into the snowdrift and make a right-angle turn in it. This makes it better and easier to put in air holes for ventilation.

A quicker snow cave can be made by digging a trench into the snow at right angles to the prevailing wind. Over the trench place boughs, ski poles, or whatever can be placed across it. Cover it all with either twigs or a poncho or something similar and heap it with a layer of snow. Leave just enough room to squeeze down into it. This will protect you from the wind if you have no other protection. The snow sides and cover will offer some insulation. Once in, try to block the air above you, but not in any way that you might smother. Try to keep cold air from seeping in.

Igloos, of course, make the best snow houses. These, however, are highly specialized. If you are interested,

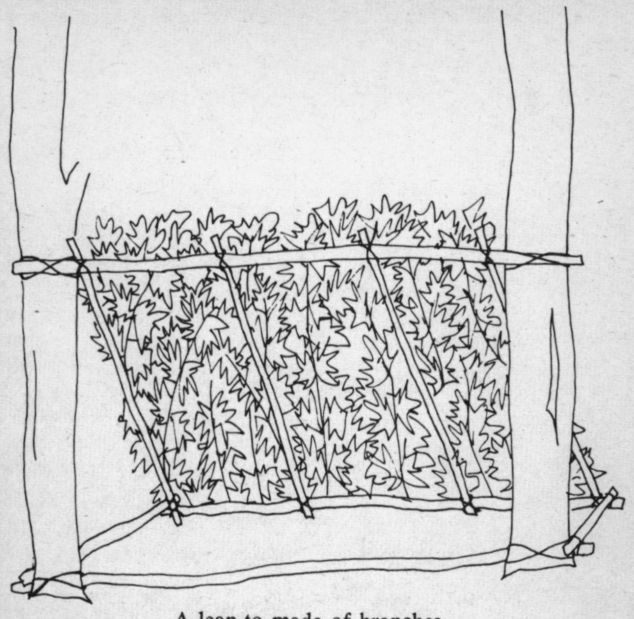

A lean-to made of branches.

learn how to make one and practice the technique. In an emergency you might find the right snow conditions, and you might have the right tools, and you might have the time to make one—but the odds are that you won't.

In a forest you can often make a shelter. The easiest to make is probably a lean-to. If you have rope with you, it will be no trick at all to make one. Find two trees about seven feet apart. Tie a branch about four feet high between them. Onto that branch pile and tie leafy branches. Put a poncho over this if you can and tie it all down. If you do not have rope, find two trees which have convenient forks where the branches meet the trunks. Place your crosspiece in the forks and proceed from there.

After blizzards, trees often have at their bases hollows in the snow, which can serve as ready-made snow caves.

Occasionally you can find good natural shelters. Large logs can often serve as the "wall" of a lean-to. If two logs have fallen so that they are parallel to each other and

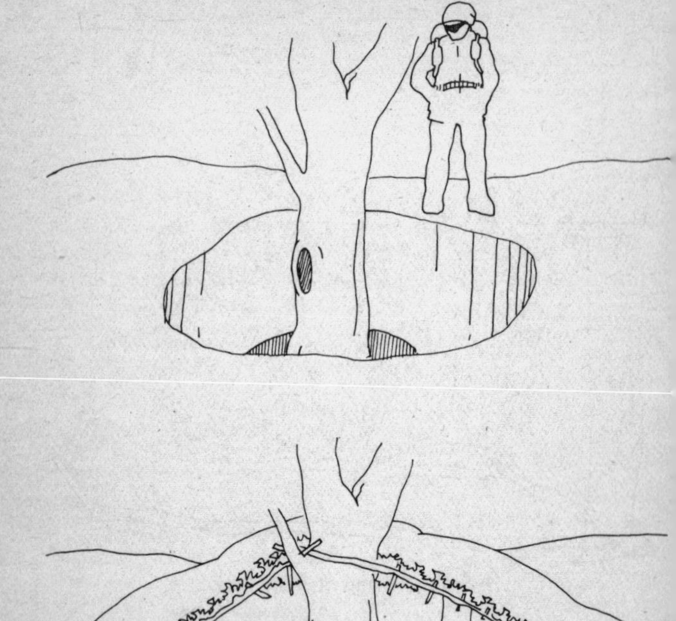

When there has been a blizzard, the wind often scoops out a place in the snow near a tree. Sometimes you can quickly make a snow shelter in such a hollow.

close together, you can place a roof over them and stay between the logs.

Many people think of caves and boulders as shelters, but they tend to be much too cold. However, they are good if—and only if—you can make a nice fire in front of them. Of course, in any cave watch out for animals.

Once you have solved the problems of your "home away from home," you should then concentrate on how to draw attention to yourself. If you have any brightly colored clothing that you can spare, try to place it where people can see it. Try to consider from what direction a search party will come and place your signal accordingly. The best place might be on top of a tree, but do not be tempted into climbing some tall tree only to fall out of it and be in a worse shape. Safety first. You might, however, find some long sturdy branch on the ground, and there may be a way of putting a red coat on it and raising the pole so it will be a flagpole.

If you have a mirror with you, you should, of course, flash it at any airplane which goes over or at people in the distance. Many "survival mirrors" have instructions for using them. If you do not have a mirror, look for something shiny—an aluminum pot, some foil, or anything else which might work.

If you do not have a mirror or something shiny, the best thing to do is to make a smoky fire. An airplane pilot can see smoke for a long distance. In fact, during the time you think people are looking for you, keep a fire ready, or at least, get all kindling and so forth ready to light at a minute's notice.

You will be in luck if there is a big snow field near you and you can get tree branches. Take the branches and, as carefully as you can, place them in the center of the snow field in the form of a big X. The clearer and bigger the better. Airplanes looking for you will no doubt see it.

All the signals above will also be useful in contacting land parties, especially if you are located in a place where you can be seen from afar.

If you see people and they do not see you, try to make some noise. If you have a whistle, blow it. Blow it three times and pause for a while. Then blow it three times again. Three of anything is a danger signal and a call for help. If you do not have a whistle, then yell, but do it correctly. Place the back of your hand over your open mouth. Yell "Wow" as loud as you can, but keep your mouth covered with your hand, then suddenly release your hand. Do this three times, then stop.

Think of ways to make noise if need be. Beat pans. Pound on a hollow log, or figure out other ways to make noises. When you sleep, you might rig up pots and pans in such a way that they keep rattling as the wind blows them together. It is sometimes remarkable how even sounds which are not very loud can carry for long distances.

When lost, keep thinking constructive thoughts. Keep trying to figure out ways of increasing your comfort and warmth. Keep planning ways to get attention. Keep making plans. Never give up. No matter how badly off you may think you are, you can bet your last dollar that other people have survived worse conditions.

20

Other Mountain Activities

Snowshoes are, of course, frameworks crisscrossed with webbing made so that you can walk on top of loose snow with them. Mountain climbers may, on occasion, have use for them. I have ascended some snow-covered peaks with them which would have been virtually impossible otherwise, and thanks to them saw some interesting sights.

There are several types of snowshoes. The type which a mountain climber would use is the bear paw, which is slightly oval. You buy them according to your weight. The heavier you are, the bigger snowshoes you need. Do not forget to add in the weight of your pack.

Even at best, bear paws are somewhat difficult to use. Their width is a nuisance. However, they have one feature which is very helpful. Of all snowshoes, they are the easiest to kick foot steps with. Secondly, being shorter than other types, they will take you straight up and down slopes better than longer ones.

There is no particular art to using snowshoes. That, in my opinion, is one of their great advantages. But, like anything, they are not perfect. Even at best, snowshoeing is slow, and from my experience, at times fatiguing.

The most important thing to know about snowshoes is how to put them on properly. The binding should be adjustable and connected correctly. You must be sure that the bindings are placed so that when you lift up your foot, the snowshoe does not tilt one way or the other. In particular, it should not tilt forward or you will be forced to lift it too high with each step, which will

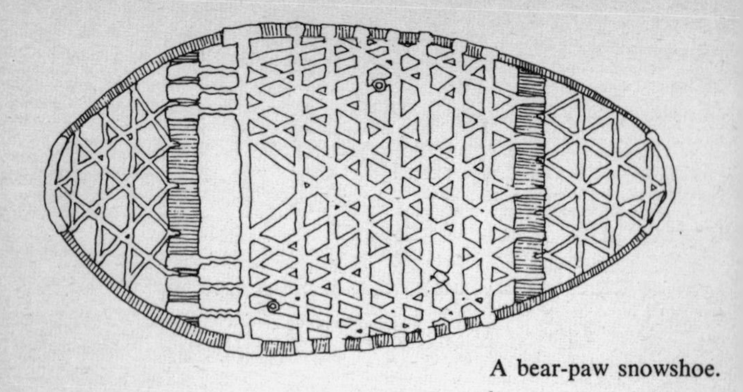

A bear-paw snowshoe.

soon exhaust you. The bindings should never cramp the feet.

Using snowshoes gives one a strange sense of confidence. It is enjoyable to go into areas which are virtually impossible to reach by hiking. In other words, they are fun and worth the effort.

There are so many excellent cameras on the market that you have a very wide choice. You cannot really say one is better than another. However, there are some things to look for. Get one which is lightweight. Try to get one which is very easy to operate. You may be using the camera when you are exhausted, will-less, and somewhat befuddled. It should be free of gadgets and things you have to think about. Since you may be taking pictures in extremely cold weather, be sure that the shutter works when the thermometer hits 50 degrees below zero or lower. Since most of your pictures will be of scenery, get a camera with a good sharp lens. I can recommend that you get a camera which does not have extremely fast speeds as you will not need them, though you would pay for them. For mountain photography you do not need a lens with a wide aperture. The aperture is indicated by "f" numbers; the smaller the number, the bigger the lens and the more expensive it will be. In mountain photography you will close the lens down. The smaller the opening, the sharper the picture, in general. For landscape photography, you can get excellent results with a medium-priced camera with a small lens and slow speeds.

In buying a camera for mountain photography, wear gloves in the store. People, of course, will think you are crazy. However, in the mountains you will be taking photographs with your gloves on. If you touch metal which is −50° F, you can run into real problems. Your skin may stick to the metal, you may get frostbite, or both. Therefore, see that you can work the camera with gloves on.

When taking mountain pictures, you will be concerned with either color or black and white film. Most people today take color photographs. On the other hand, black and white photographs can be striking. As a personal thing, I often like them better. At any rate, if you take black and white pictures, take along some filters. When I took pictures in the Colorado Rockies, I found that one of the best filters was a dark orange filter, a "G" filter. It did exactly what I wanted. It darkened the sky and made it more natural looking than you can get with just black and white film. It picked up snow shadows beautifully and made the snow look gray and textured, as it really is. Without such a filter, the sky is too light and the snow lacks texture and often looks chalky and lacking in any details. A red "A" filter, which is sometimes used, darkens the sky even more and darkens all the shadows on the snow so that they look too dark. Pictures taken with an "A" filter look fake. They make the snow look harder than it really is.

It is sometimes fun to overdo the whole thing, however. If you use infrared film and a red filter you can get amazing, though really fake results. Trees will look white and the sky pitch black. You may wonder, why do it? Infrared will cut through haze. Peaks miles and miles away, which may look somewhat hazy to the naked eye, will show up in detail on infrared film. It is an amazing film that way.

Polaroid filters are like Polaroid sunglasses. Sometimes, especially when there is snow around, the glare in the mountains can be too much. A picture of a scene will look hazy. A Polaroid filter will cut through the haze and glare. With it you can take a picture and get details which would otherwise be lost. A Polaroid filter can be used with both black and white film and with color shots.

In taking landscape shots it is usually best to set the "f" number for the largest number practical, such as f16 or f22. Using an f22 number and a "G" filter, you can usually take a picture of a bright sunlit scene at 1/50 of a second. If you are standing, do not try to take a picture at a slower speed, or the movement of your body will cause the picture to blur a bit. Stand with your legs slightly apart, push the camera against your face (unless it is too cold). Stand as still as you can. Do not breathe. Slowly and smoothly push the shutter release. If wind is not rocking you back and forth, the shot should be clear and not fuzzy. If there is a wind blowing, take the picture at a higher speed and change the other settings to compensate.

Of course, many cameras today are automatic and you cannot change the settings. However, be sure that the original setting is correct for the film used and for the filter.

In taking mountain photographs, do not try for panoramas. Though huge vistas are impressive to look at, they hardly ever come out effectively in a photograph. It is usually best to photograph old dead trees, unusual rock formations, wildflowers, and so on rather than take "big" mountain pictures. If you take pictures of people, do not just group them all together and have them look at the camera. Try to photograph activities. Show your friends making a campfire, pounding a piton into a rock, rappelling, and so on. Such photographs are far more interesting to look at. When I worked in a photography shop in Colorado, I saw literally thousands of photographs people had taken of the mountains. Take it from me, most were no good, because people always tried to photograph peaks and vistas.

It is my belief that good climbers have an almost intuitive feeling about nature. They understand, as the old saying goes, the lay of the land. They can look at a valley and know where a lake will be located. They can look at a cliff and tell what sort of handholds it will have. If they see a limestone ridge on one side of a mountain, they can pretty well guess where it will be on the other side. Such an insight at first seems remarkable. Yet it is not. It is learned.

Real nature study, thus, goes beyond what is discussed on a picnic. For mountain climbers it can be of survival interest. The subject is so wide and of such scope that no one could begin to describe it in a few pages. However, I will leave you with some insights into how it can be practical. A spring with no animal tracks around it and no insects may be poisonous. Rocks which form steep cliffs in one area are almost sure to do the same someplace else, and a general view of the land will show you where that "someplace else" is located. Some plants indicate water, and some indicate dryness. A greenish color in the northern sky is a good indication that colder weather is on the way. It is amazing how helpful such knowledge can be. Moreover, the knowledge can be of lifetime interest. Knowledge learned outdoors sticks with you for a much longer time than book knowledge.

Not only will nature studies help you climb better, but they will make your trip more pleasant. For example, some wood, such as piñon wood, gives off marvelously scented smoke when burned. It is better to climb a cliff where there are highly colored rocks than another one, as color indicates minerals. Who knows what nice semi-precious gem might be found while climbing? Mountain climbers in Rocky Mountain National Park are often rewarded by seeing a very rare rosy finch, found almost nowhere else in all the world. High-altitude climbing made it possible for me to see a comet (the only one I ever saw) which was virtually impossible for people to see at sea-level elevations.

Always learn as much as you can. Learn especially to be observant. Do not climb just so that later on you can say, "I climbed such and such peak." There are some people who are peak baggers. They push up a mountain or cliff and see nothing to the right or to the left. They have one goal in mind—either a summit or the conquest of a route. There is much more to climbing than that. There is a total experience. Some people seem to feel that mountains are "conquered," but of course the only thing which is really conquered is something within ourselves.

Some have found a beauty in the hills that they never dreamed existed. Others have found that in climbing they overcame fears—and, yes, even a certain laziness. Others have discovered nature, for it was the first time that they ever saw a real wilderness area. Others have found that the mountains opened them up in terms of mental awareness.

Many climbers have said that the tension and deep concentration needed for climbing, especially under dangerous conditions, have made them far more aware of the world than they had ever been before. Their minds suddenly absorbed much more than before. Such climbers have, for example, seen the world about them with a vividness they never before experienced. Rocks, crystal grains, the shape, textures, and colors of lichens have suddenly become apparent to them as though their eyes became hundreds of times sharper and their minds many times more aware. At times like that, a mountain climber will suddenly realize who he really is.

It cannot, of course, be stressed too much that litter and pollution will destroy much that is wonderful in the mountains. All climbers should help preserve the purity of the natural environment. They should also remember that the ecology of the mountains is frail and easily damaged. Plants and animals live under extremely harsh conditions. Life destroyed in the mountains will not spring back as easily as it does in some areas of the world. Plants and animals can easily become extinct. Mountain meadows—and what is more lovely than an alpine pasture—can erode quickly if too many people tramp through them. Once eroded, they never return. A flower which is picked is not just one flower. Each flower has hundreds of seeds and thousands of pollen grains, so you are actually picking dozens of flowers and spoiling future generations.

Climbers, in my opinion, are serious and privileged people. They have learned methods for entering into the wildest and least touched of all areas of the earth. They need therefore to be responsible to see that their technology does not destroy what is there. In this respect though, I think that climbers have, in general, been a most considerate group. I know of many places where many climbers have been but which are still remarkably untouched and which look as they did before anyone ever arrived there. In my opinion, that is one of the ultimate signs of good mountain climbers.

21

Knots for Mountain Climbers

There are several knots which a mountain climber needs to know. It is extremely important that any and all knots used be tied correctly. A rope is no stronger than the knot in it. A knot which comes loose can obviously be extremely dangerous.

The secret to understanding knots is to know a *few* knots well. It is far better to be able to tie accurately four or five kinds of knots in high winds, while fatigued, or even in the dark than to be able to tie a couple of dozen "fancy" knots.

Elsewhere in this book, the overhand, figure-eight, prusik, fisherman's, and bowline knots have been described. Here are some more knots that can come in handy.

THE OVERHAND KNOT IN A LOOP

An overhand knot is a simple knot to make. It can easily be made in a loop of rope. It will secure the loop and the loop will not slip loose.

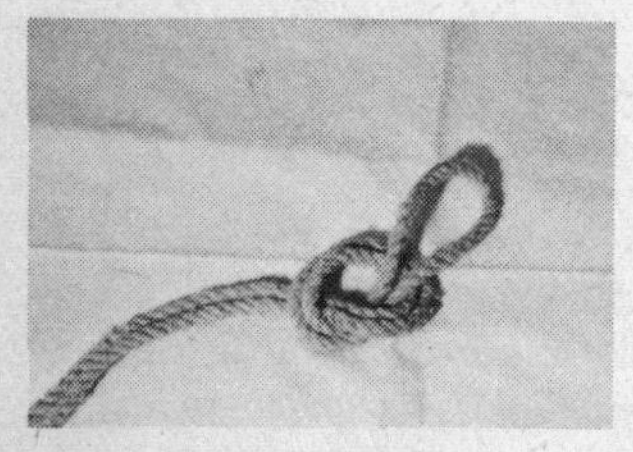

Overhand knot in a loop. (*Photograph by the author*)

THE TWO-HALF-HITCH KNOT

This knot is used for belays. The climber who is belaying another takes the climbing rope and puts it through a carabiner attached to a piton solidly placed in a rock crack. After that, he takes the rope and makes a loop in it. He ties the loop to the seven-rope waist band with a two-half-hitch knot.

The two-half-hitch knot is also useful when used on a single rope for tying things, such as a tent rope to a tree.

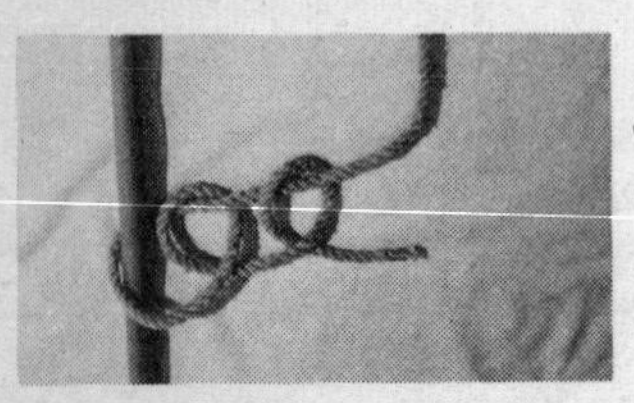

The two-half-hitch knot. (*Photograph by the author*)

THE DOUBLE FISHERMAN'S KNOT

This knot is really a fisherman's knot made with two loops instead of one. It is preferable to the fisherman's knot as it is stronger and will not pull out as easily. Use it on the seven-loop waist band. It is, however, slightly more difficult to tie. Be sure it sets when pulled together.

You might wonder why this knot used for mountain climbing is called a fisherman's knot. Long before nylon ropes were invented, fishermen used this knot to tie slippery gut leaders together. Those leaders were like nylon rope in many ways.

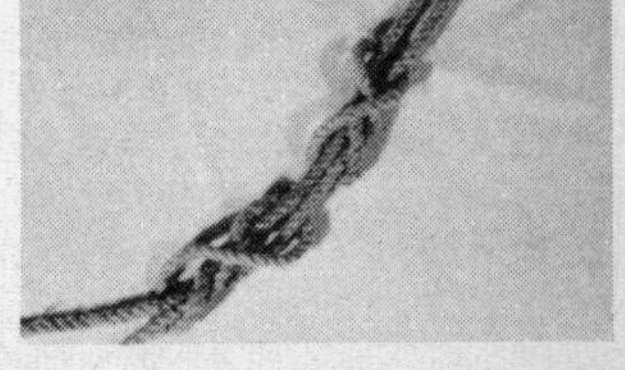

The double fisherman's knot. (*Photograph by Alexander Smith*)

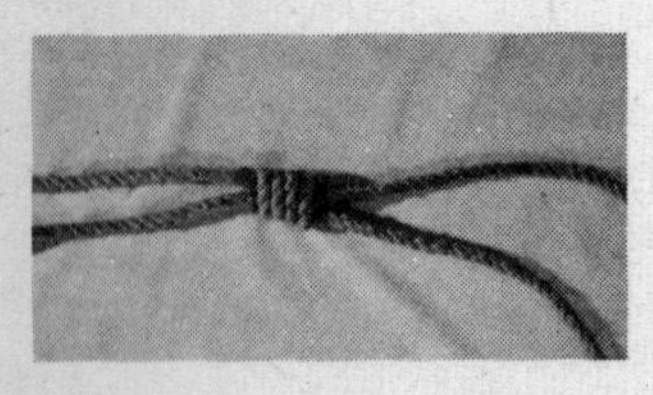

The double fisherman's knot tightened. Notice how it should fit together smoothly. (*Photograph by Alexander Smith*)

THE REEF KNOT OR SQUARE KNOT

The reef knot, universally used for tying two ropes of the same diameter together, is not a particularly good climbing knot. It has to be made exactly right. There is always the chance someone will tie a "granny" knot, which looks like a reef knot. It can also come apart on slippery nylon rope. Use it only for tying knots in knapsacks and in places where there is no danger. In situations like that it is a good knot to use, as you can quickly make it and quickly untie it. In fact, sailors centuries ago discovered it was the perfect knot for quickly tying reef points in sails and untying them. But do not use the knot where your life depends on it.

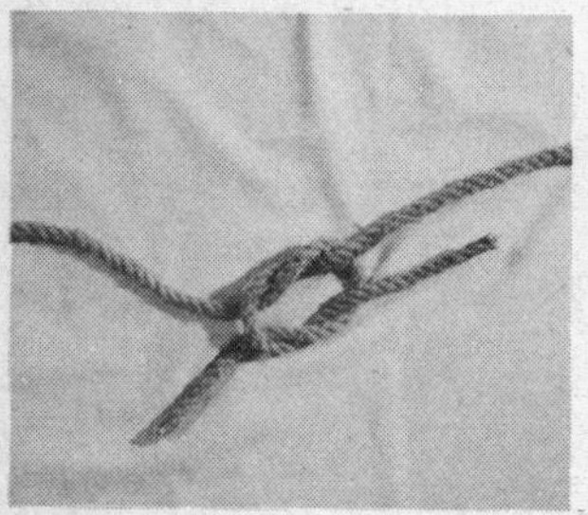

The reef or square knot. Note carefully the positions of the loops and ends of the ropes. (*Photograph by Alexander Smith*)

THE TENT GUY KNOT OR TAUT LINE HITCH

This knot is used for tent guys. The convenient thing about the knot is that, if you use natural fiber ropes for the tent guys, you can loosen or tighten the rope at will. That really makes a big difference.

The tent guy knot. (*Photograph by the author*)

THE FISHERMAN'S BLOOD KNOT

If you need to tie two nylon cords together, it is useful to use a fisherman's blood knot, as nylon cord will not slip with it. This knot, of course, is not a climbing knot but is only shown here for camping purposes. The same knot can also be used as a hitch, as shown.

The fisherman's blood knot. (*Photograph by the author*)

The fisherman's blood knot used as a hitch. (*Photograph by the author*)

THE CLOVE HITCH

This is a convenient knot to use for tying tent cords to trees. Any camper should know it, though it has no use in mountain climbing itself.

The clove hitch. (*Photograph by the author*)

22

Check Lists

Check lists are very handy. Before going on any trip, even a day trip, make out a check list and see to it that each item listed on it is taken. That way nothing will accidentally be left behind. Once you have gained some experience, you will be able to make out your own check list. Until then it might be handy for you if one is provided. Remember that all people are individuals and that each person will bring on a trip a slightly different assortment of items than other people. Thus, no check list will serve all people. Moreover, each trip is slightly different, and therefore different items will be taken. So do not follow the lists slavishly, but take them as suggestions and use them as you see fit.

A CHECK LIST FOR A DAY ROCK CLIMB IN THE SUMMERTIME

1. Climbing boots with shoelaces in good order.
2. A pair of woolen socks and a pair of silk socks to wear underneath them.
3. Climbing pants such as knickers (never blue jeans).
4. Any comfortable shirt.
5. A good tough jacket, such as a canvas one, which will prevent rope burns.
6. A sweater.
7. A knit wool cap.
8. A rock climbing helmet.

9. Two pairs of gloves—one pair leather for protection against rope burns, and the other woolen fingerless gloves.
10. Nylon rope, about 7⁄16 inch in diameter and from 100 to 150 feet in length.
11. A manila rope long enough to go seven times around the waist, or a climbing harness.
12. A carabiner with a screw that keeps the gate shut.
13. A piton hammer and enough pitons and carabiners for the climb.
14. A shoulder rope for carrying the "hardware," meaning the pitons, carabiners, and so on.
15. About thirty feet of nylon rope 7⁄16 inch in diameter for slings.
16. A snake-bite kit.
17. A first aid kit.
18. A knapsack.
19. A canteen filled with water, maybe with a cup.
20. Food. For a day trip most people take along sandwiches, an orange, some chocolate bars. Take whatever appeals to you and don't worry much about weight.
21. A rain poncho.

A CHECK LIST FOR A ROCK AND/OR SNOW AND ICE CLIMB IN THE WINTER

Take along the items listed above, but add to them the following:

1. Long underwear.
2. A woolen shirt. If you are like me and cannot stand wool next to your skin, wear a cotton shirt under it.
3. A Dacron- or down-filled parka with a hood.
4. Mittens. These are not worn while climbing but can be put on during rest stops.
5. A tough outer parka which can take rope burns.
6. Goggles.
7. An ice axe, if needed.
8. Crampons, if needed.

9. Ice pitons, if needed.
10. A snow deadman, if needed.
11. Woolen scarves.
12. A sleeping bag, in case someone suffers from the cold.
13. In addition to the food carried in summertime, carry along a can of condensed milk for hypothermia (not as a snack, as tasty as it is).
14. A handwarmer, which is a luxury item.
15. A face mask.

A CHECK LIST FOR A FIVE-DAY CAMPING AND MOUNTAIN CLIMBING TRIP

This check list is not connected with the check lists above but is to be used by itself.

1. A good pair of all-around mountain climbing boots—probably medium weight, but it will depend on the type of terrain you expect to cross.
2. Some people take lightweight slippers or mukluks for use around the camp. I never do, but there could be advantages to them.
3. Three pairs of woolen and nylon socks of smooth weave.
4. Three pairs of white silk socks.
5. One pair of sturdy trousers. Except in a very warm climate, they should be wool and Dacron, or one hundred per cent wool, of appropriate weight.
6. Wear one pair of underpants on the first day out, and carry four more, thus having a clean pair for each day.
7. If you like undershirts, take three along. Fishnet tee shirts are the best.
8. Women sometimes like to wear halters on the trail.
9. Depending on the weather conditions you will face, take along some combination of sweaters, parka shell, and/or a down- or Dacron-filled parka.

10. For campfires carry a pair of cheapo canvas gloves with leather palms.
11. Two brightly colored bandanas.
12. Two pairs of goggles.
13. Appropriate hats—a wide-brimmed one for hiking in the woods, and a warmer one for high peaks.
14. If needed, mosquito netting for the broad-brimmed hat.
15. Extra shoelaces.

TOILET ITEMS

1. Toothbrush.
2. Use salt for toothpaste, or carry tooth powder, which is a little extra weight. Do not carry toothpaste.
3. Biodegradable soap.
4. Possibly a washcloth.
5. A roll of toilet paper.
6. A comb.

IN A FIRST AID KIT BOX

1. Tweezers.
2. A small pair of scissors, mainly for cutting moleskin.
3. Moleskin.
4. A snake-bite kit. This goes into the bigger kit.
5. Aspirin.
6. Salt tablets.
7. A magnifying glass for slivers.
8. Adhesive tape, probably one inch wide and five yards long.
9. Band-Aids.
10. About five three-by-three-inch sterile gauze pads.
11. An antiseptic ointment, such as Bacitracin.
12. Labiosan or another good lip ointment.
13. Ointment to screen ultraviolet rays for the skin.
14. Insect repellent, if needed.

15. Coconut oil for dry skin, if desired.
16. Talcum powder or cornstarch for chafing, if needed.
17. Antihistamines for allergies, if needed.
18. Laxatives of the type one chews.
19. A burn ointment.
20. A general antibiotic bought with a doctor's prescription if you will be in really difficult country where it is next to impossible to get quick help.
21. Any regular prescription medicine you use. Be sure to ask your doctor about the effect of your medicines when taken at high altitude and/or in extremely cold weather.
22. A lightweight but good first aid book.

REPAIR AND SEWING KIT

1. A small container of waterproof salve for the boots. Be sure that you take the right sort as different types are used for leathers which are tanned differently. When you buy the boots, ask the salesman what sort of salve to use. If you forget, take your boots to a good shoe repairman and ask him what to use.
2. Repair tape for nylon. This is useful for rips in clothing, sleeping bags, and tents.
3. Safety pins.
4. A small sewing kit with needles. The needles can also be used for getting out slivers.
5. I always carried some rawhide thongs about forty inches long. Today most people carry about one hundred feet of ⅛-inch nylon cord, which is handy.

MAPS, COMPASS, NOTEBOOK, ETC.

1. A good sturdy compass.
2. A topographic map of the region.
3. A smaller map to fit in a shirt pocket.
4. A pencil or two.

5. A small notebook. Write in it the time of sunrise and sunset for the places you will be; also the rising and setting times of the moon, and, if possible, of the planets.
6. A lightweight six-inch plastic ruler. This is not necessary, but it can be handy.

KNIFE, WHISTLE, SIGNAL MIRROR

1. A simple, sturdy jackknife, preferably with a metal loop so you can tie it to your belt by a cord.
2. A small sharpening stone.
3. A loud whistle, such as a police whistle.
4. A signal mirror if you will be in a really wild area.
5. A waterproof matchbox with matches. Plenty of other matches as well.

COOKING EQUIPMENT

1. A stove. If you take along food which does not require any cooking, you can, of course, leave this at home.
2. A fuel bottle for the stove, the fuel, the primer fuel, and the eyedropper for it.
3. A funnel for pouring the fuel into the stove.
4. A set of nesting pots, pans, and dishes.
5. A cup, which is carried on the outside of the pack.
6. A spoon, which is needed. A fork, which is not really needed. An extra knife is good so the jackknife does not get all gummed up with food.

FOOD

See the chapter on food; the items are too varied for a check list.

WATER

1. A canteen for carrying.
2. If there is a large group, one person should carry along a collapsible plastic water jug.
3. Halazone tablets for purifying water.

LIGHT

A flashlight and batteries, or a carbide lamp with fuel.

TENT

1. A tent.
2. Tent accessories, such as ropes, poles, pegs and so on, plus a sack.
3. A snow shovel.
4. A whisk broom.

SLEEPING BAG

1. One or two sleeping bags as needed.
2. The sleeping-bag cover if it has one.
3. A ground cloth, if needed.
4. Mosquito netting, if needed.
5. An insulation pad or air mattress, if needed.
6. A stuff sack for the sleeping bag.

THE PACK

1. This is an impossible item to forget.
2. Be sure all of its needed belts, straps, and so on are in good shape and also carried.
3. A day pack. One is often carried on top of a regular pack.

PERSONAL ITEMS

1. A wallet.
2. Identification.
3. Tetanus-shot instructions and blood type.
4. Driver's license.
5. Emergency addresses.
6. Money.
7. Telephone change.
8. Passport, if needed.
9. A waterproof bag for wallet, papers, and/or passport.

CLIMBING EQUIPMENT

The climbing equipment, of course, will be carefully chosen for the type of rock, snow, and ice you expect to encounter. A check list is impossible to make out ahead of time. But the following might help.

1. A nylon climbing rope in perfect condition, 7⁄16 inch thick and 100 to 150 feet long.
2. Manila rope for waist bands.
3. A one-inch-diameter nylon rope if you are going to cross a glacier. It should be about 100 feet long.
4. 7⁄16-inch-diameter nylon rope for slings.
5. A 500-foot ¼-inch rappel rope, if needed.
6. Rock climbing helmet, if needed.
7. One screw-type carabiner.
8. As many carabiners as needed.
9. As many pitons as needed.
10. A piton hammer.
11. An ice axe.
12. Crampons, if needed.
13. Prusik-knot slings, if needed.
14. Carabiner pulleys, if needed.
15. Ice pitons and a snow deadman if needed.
16. Avalanche cord, if needed.
17. Snowshoes or skis if needed, and of course, all the bindings, fake fur and so forth, plus ski wax.

MISCELLANEOUS ITEMS

1. Wristwatch.
2. If possible carry at least one nature guide along for studying trees, flowers, and so forth.
3. A small transistor radio. Nothing is worse than listening to a radio in a campground or on a trail. I would never suggest it, except that you can use it for weather reports.
4. A camera is not a necessary piece of equipment, but I strongly recommend that you take one along. Carry along all the needed film, filters, and so forth.
5. It is sometimes very pleasant to go fishing, especially on an extended trip. If it appeals to you, take along all the necessary items, plus a fishing license.

Index